HOW TO

PROFIT

FROM THE
NEXT GREAT
DEPRESSION

DR. JOHN L. KING

A SIGNET BOOK

NEW AMERICAN LIBRARY

A DIVISION OF PENGUIN BOOKS USA INC.

This book previously appeared in an NAL Books edition published
by New American Library and published simultaneously in
Canada by Penguin Books Canada Limited.

SIGNET, SIGNET CLASSIC, MENTOR, ONYX, PLUME, MERIDIAN
and NAL BOOKS are published by New American Library,
a division of Penguin Books USA Inc.
1633 Broadway, New York, New York 10019

First Signet Printing, June, 1989

1 2 3 4 5 6 7 8 9

To John R., Debra, and Cameron King

ACKNOWLEDGMENTS

The original idea for this book began more than ten years ago when I discovered that textbook economic ideas, even basic banking theory, fit poorly with today's world and the way we live in it. Accepted ideas failed to account for events that were going on around us on a daily basis. This led to many years of historical research and reading and, finally, to the book.

My thanks go to my agent, Ben Kamsler, a man of vision and patience; to April Rhodes in California, who so competently put the manuscript together through many changes; and to Michaela Hamilton, my New York editor, who followed Emerson's dictums on new ideas and their influence on people's minds: "The more unusual the thought, the more important it is likely to be." I also thank the many loyal readers of my newsletter, "Future Economic Trends" who have learned, as I have, from the lessons of economic history.

CONTENTS

"By the Law of Periodical Repetition, everything which has happened once must happen again and again and again—and not capriciously, but at regular periods, and each thing in its own period, not another's, and each obeying its own law . . . and the same Nature which delights in periodical repetition in the skies is the Nature which orders the affairs of the earth. Let us not underrate the value of that hint."

Mark Twain

PREFACE TO PAPERBACK EDITION

The simple message of this book is to explain how the excessive use of credit in America—for a very long time—will inevitably plunge us into a very long depression. This is because one great lesson of history is that debts are always paid. Unfortunately, in our time they will be paid in defaults, foreclosures, repossessions, etc., and not in cash.

All through economic history the historic solution to excessive debt has been its forced liquidation. Not an easy path.

The growing weakness of credit in 1988 was appearing in the media in the fall of 1988: *Newsweek*, in a cover story, November 6, 1988, headlined "The Latin Debt Crisis Grows Worse After 8 Years. Does Anyone Have An Answer?" And the *Wall Street Journal* on November 6, 1988, ran a lengthy article on growing auto repossessions, which by that time had reached historic high levels in America. Those who bought cars when interest rates were lowered by the auto companies (to stimulate sales) were trapped and unable to repay their loans. In this book I had predicted this train of events would happen. There will be more signs of credit weakness as our banks and savings and loan institutions also contract.

The growing financial weakness is most often evident when a money panic appears. That is a time when the stock market falls sharply, perhaps more than it did on October 19, 1987, and interest rates soar, etc. And this time, uniquely, the U.S. dollar will also tumble in world markets, reflecting a financially weak America. Like England did in the 1930s when it went off the sterling standard, so in America in the days ahead, the world will abandon the U.S. dollar as the world's reserve currency. Another signal of the end of America's financial and industrial leadership.

The money panic will also bring with it frozen credit-card use, real estate prices tumbling, and, perhaps, withdrawals being limited at banks and thrifts . . . a period of turmoil and distress for all Americans.

One of the main messages of this book is that readers should again become self-reliant and not harbor false hopes that the federal government can solve these problems for us. No institution can resist the forces of price deflation and falling values. From the beginning of economic time no one has been able to prevent this happening, and now is no different.

Paper assets such as mortgages, certificates of deposit, mutual funds, and so on will, as time progresses, go back to their original form, worthless paper, and nothing can halt this trend.

Hard times will probably emerge by late 1989.

And the bad news is that they will last for a long time. Most people have forgotten that the first Great Depression actually lasted for ten years, and only World War II ended it. The suffering that happened during that ten-year period has also been long forgotten.

The urgent message in this book is to get ready now for a future that is already writ in stone. Our standard of living will fall sharply and we will get used to living on less and with less.

We are on the cutting edge of a major change in America and change is an ordeal. It will bring fear and a feeling of lost security to most of us. A large segment of the population will simply rebel at this turn of events. And, that will bring still more change.

This root change in our life-styles will be broad and will bring an upheaval in the way we do things—new business forms will emerge, a movement to rural areas for living will also occur, and other transformations will follow insuring that the future will be very different from the past we are all so familiar with.

But our new future, though vastly different, will be a personally rewarding one, and one with bona-fide joy and triumph that is bound to rise from the ashes, like Phoenix. If you are prudent and patient you will be able to fashion a better life for yourself and your family. Have faith that tomorrow will, truly, be better since it will. That is also a crucial lesson of history.

—John L. King
Santa Barbara, CA
November 1988

PREFACE

No subject in economics provokes a greater variety of conflicting opinions than that of financial crises and periods of depression. Numerous explanations of their causes have been advanced, and most of them demonstrate irreconcilable differences.

In our time, there is a large brick wall dividing these irreconcilable opinions on whether or not there can be a depression. On the side of no-depression-ever are academic economists, government economists and the vast majority of financial writers in the media, newspapers and magazines. They have constructed clever defenses to justify their beliefs and they, of course, have a deep vested interest in maintaining the status quo, the conventional wisdom and mainstream notions. I have had to deal with them on radio talk shows, and their euphoria is a thing to behold. There is a smaller group who sit on the other side of the wall and are convinced a depression is now inevitable, which make authorities powerless . . . soon. I am on that side.

If you are an ordinary mortal, however, and have witnessed the cycles in the weather, in nature and in man, it seems reasonable to you, I feel confident, to assume that cycles also occur in business activity. Most of you reading this have probably lived long enough to remember ups and downs in the rhythm of your own business and financial affairs.

The direction of this book is totally to the public and not written to jibe with the other side of the economic wall and those who have ideas that can be likened to a steel trap. They will promise you tirelessly that we cannot have another depression and, in the same breath, promise you that your savings are insured in your bank. Time will prove both of these ideas to be totally false and fatal to your financial well-being as well.

How bad will the time we are entering be? Clemént Juglar, a respected French financial writer and economist, wrote as far back as 1889, and it is still true today, "Paradoxical as it may seem, the riches of nations can be measured by the violence of the crises which they experience."[1] You have heard again and again that America is the richest nation ever on the face of the earth. This is probably true if you are counting material things. Therefore, fasten your seat belt. Juglar's idea is precise: we will experience the most violent crises in America, and in the world, that have ever been seen. That is a promise and a certainty.

I believe the cause of the coming depression will be the mountain of debt we have accumulated since 1945. The whole country: individuals, federal government, cities and states, and corporations are laboring under this incredible debt load. Not only that, the debt carries with it perhaps the highest interest rates, for a continued period, in all of economic history. In addition, as you will read, we have entered—I know this is hard to believe—a period of falling prices. Falling prices bring lower cash flows, less income and therefore less ability to pay debt with its interest, which compounds while we all sleep. Wages, too, are in steep decline.

The great instrument which created this nightmare is credit. Our abuse of it will change our economic future forever.

I do not know when this crisis will happen. No one does. But the down wave we are in is intensifying and accelerating, and there is no way it can be reversed by the government, by our economic theories, by anything. The die is cast. We will crash into the worst economic times imaginable!

Therefore, I urge you to bite the bullet. Realize this inevitability and prepare for it now. Be one minute early rather than one minute late.

Financial crises and subsequent depressions are older than our economic system. They go back to very early times. Why is this? Because human behavior is the one constant that never changes. We will soon see again that those reared on envy and greed can, and will, grow up to be desperate and dangerous citizens. So, we will be hit economically, politically and socially—all at the same time.

A
"FICTIONAL"
INTRODUCTION

The Secret of Surviving the Crisis

Anytown, USA
A Quiet Sunday Evening

John and Mary Comfortable are spending a quiet evening in their $145,000 split-level tract home. The children are watching a television show while John and Mary discuss the family finances—combined income of $45,000, $1,800 in their checking account and $1,200 in a savings & loan. Although their five credit cards are extended to the limits with payments totaling $1,000 a month, John's new car payment runs $350 a month and the mortgage is starting to choke them, they still feel confident about the future. Mary has been promised a promotion, John is up for a healthy raise and so they turn in for the night with rosy thoughts of tomorrow.

The tomorrow of their dreams never comes!
Tomorrow the nightmare of The Panic
hits them—right between the eyes.

The Next Morning

The Comfortable family, along with everyone in America, wake up to an alarming report on the radio. *"We interrupt this hour of recorded music to bring you a news flash. The New York stock market opened down 110 points and is still falling. Rumors have it that the foreign central banks have withdrawn massive deposits from U.S. banks, and the world banking system is at the brink."*

John and Mary stand transfixed by the radio, unwilling to believe what they have just heard. Then, another news flash.

"Gold is up $75 in the first hour of trading and interest rates have risen five points in an hour. The prime rate is now at 12% and rising! We repeat, a financial crisis is underway."

Realizing the need for fast action, the Comfortables decide that John will go to the bank while Mary heads for the savings & loan. If they withdraw all their money from both institutions, they figure they can at least stock up on food and gasoline.

By the time John reaches the bank at 9:30, the line is two blocks long. New rumors are traveling like an uncontrollable fire through the waiting ranks. *"The bank is busted. Foreigners have withdrawn every penny of their $280 billion in U.S. bank deposits. The President and the Secretary of the Treasury are preparing an order to declare an immediate bank holiday."*

At 9:45, one of the men in line turns up his portable radio for an announcement. *"The Pres-*

ident has declared a state of national emergency. All banks and S&Ls are to be closed immediately, along with the stock and commodity exchanges. All wire transfers of funds, both international and national, are to be frozen. Credit cards are frozen. Stay tuned for additional announcements."

The crowd goes crazy. People pushing and shoving, terrified because their funds are frozen. All anyone has to spend is what they have in their pockets.

John rushes home and meets his wife, who is in a state of panic from her fruitless trip to the savings & loan. "What will we do now?" she cries. "We only have $35 cash between us!" "We'll use what we have for food," John says, realizing he is grasping at straws.

They rush to the market, but find the shelves almost empty. Others have preceded them. They leave to find gasoline for the car, but find the station closed. There has already been a run on gasoline which wiped out the station's reserves. They return home, dejected and terrified. More news alerts bombard them.

"Gold is up to $900 an ounce, stocks are down over 400 points on a volume of 400 million shares. And interest rates are still soaring. The prime rate is now 18%. Chaos reigns in the world's financial markets and Mexico has just announced she will default on her $100 billion world debt."

John and Mary gather their children to them and try to figure out what has happened to their middle-class world. There doesn't seem to be any logical way to explain the devastation to the youngsters; they barely understand it themselves.

The Following Day

The bad news intensifies. Stocks have fallen 1200 points, gold is $1,800 an ounce, the banks and S&Ls remain closed and now there are occasional power outages to add to the misery. Few people venture out on the streets; those who do are looking for food, even if it means resorting to criminal activity. Everyone is terrified and rightly so.

"If this is not Doomsday," John, now in total depression, says to his wife as she lies nearly unconscious on their bed after surreptitiously taking a handful of sleeping pills, "it's a good substitute." John has, at that point, no idea of the greater tragedy ahead but already he blames himself. He has believed the media and the politicians up to now and has forgotten the biblical warning, "Men are trapped when bad times suddenly come." He now knows that he and his family are trapped like tigers in a cage, stripped of their freedom, their very life!

Sound like a movie plot? It isn't!
It's a potential real-life drama and
it could happen sooner than we think!

The Point of the Story

The crisis is inevitable. We know that from economic history. But you can escape unscathed. The secret is to be ready—you must be one minute early and not one minute late to avoid getting trapped. You must have your assets stored where you can get to them quickly and easily.

INTRODUCTION

Emerson wrote, "The more unusual the thought, the more important it is likely to be, for the world is more in need of new ideas than anything else."

I hope you will find some new ideas in this book.

World War II was a watershed for us in America. After the war we saw the growth of suburbia, vast new technologies, a rapid growth in international trade and, for my business—economics—a great shift in thinking.

This change in economic thinking was initiated at the University of Chicago in 1940 when a group of economists and statisticians got together and invented a brand-new way of thinking about economics. Their new theory was nurtured and fed by mathematicians. By 1945 it had blossomed forth as "econometrics." Maybe this doesn't seem like much of a change to you, but, believe me, it greatly altered the way we look at economic events. The ideas of such economic philosophers as Joseph Schumpeter, John Stuart Mill and a long line of others were largely abandoned. And the teaching of economic history at the university level was generally discontinued in 1945.

U.S. economic ideas today are a product of forty odd years of this new, unhistorical, mathematical approach. If you want to study economics today, you had better plan on becoming a mathematician first. This is an important break with the past. The contrast between the historical economist and the current mathematical economist is stark. The economy does not behave according to predictable numbers and computer printouts. It is ruled by people with emotional reactions to worldly events and therefore cannot be analyzed by numbers only. A wide spectrum of factors must be taken into consideration.

Some years ago when I was in Southern California, I hired a newly minted Ph.D. from the University of Pennsylvania who had been teaching for a few years before he joined me. He told me he could just as easily have taken his Ph.D. in mathematics as in economics. During our first week together, I gave him 15 classic books on economic history to read. He carefully put them on one corner of his desk, where they remained until he left to go abroad a year later. For him the lessons of economic history held no interest at all, which is how it is for many or most of the one hundred and fifty thousand Ph.D. mathematical economists out there now—very different from the less than one thousand historical economists, like myself.

Not that all of them believe mathematics has all that much value. According to David Walsh

in his book *The Idea of Economic Complexity*,
Paul Samuelson of MIT, a Nobel Prize-winning
economist, "joked that it was so odd to find
himself working on 'turnpike' theorems and os-
culating envelopes; nonsubstitutability relations
in Minoski-Ricado-Leontief-Metzler metrics of
Mosak-Hicks type."[1]

Now, if you think about the positively terrible
forecasting record evidenced by all econometric
models, and the mathematicians' inability to
develop ideas that the public can understand,
what we have here is a sorry mess.

"The outside world's discontentment with the
role of the economist appears to be reaching
inside the profession." So wrote Leonard Silk,
economic expert of the *New York Times* in January 1985, after attending the annual conven-
tion of the American Economic Association in
Dallas, Texas.[2] He went on to note that the
reason for this discontentment was not likely
to change soon, however. It's become the established way. So the bright-eyed, shiny young
faces who have arisen lately as our popular
brand-new experts will continue to dominate
economic thinking into the foreseeable future.
Their eagerness to lecture, to stand before us
and dispense their enthusiasms, is a product
of their youthful inexperience and lack of historical knowledge.

I am from the old school. I got my feet wet in
economics at the Wharton School before World
War II. What was taught in those days was
economic history—plus, of course, the ideas of
the great economic philosophers of the past. I
loved this course of study, and was good at it.

In my senior year I was nominated to Beta Gamma Sigma, the business school's Phi Beta Kappa. And I graduated fourth in my class of over 400.

After some years in various jobs, I returned to graduate school while teaching students in junior colleges and universities throughout California. I taught economic theory, economic history, banking, business cycles, investments and continued to read economic history relentlessly. While at graduate school working on my Ph.D. degree, I launched my newsletter, "Future Economic Trends." That was over seventeen years ago and it's still going strong today. Accompanying each of those early newsletters was a lengthy essay on parallels to be found in economic history.

So, you see, it is this long and exhaustive research of economic history and related fields that causes me to call the present state of the economy a crisis.

Debt and Its Interest

The Federal Reserve Bank of New York reported in 1986 that the total domestic debt was $8.2 trillion. But by 1987, in the *Economic Report* of the President, total domestic debt had reached $11.06 trillion.[3] Assume an interest rate on this debt of 10 percent. This means the annual interest rate paid by American consumers would be $1.1 trillion for one year and the same amount, and more, the next year. The price of credit-based prosperity comes very high.

How did we pay this amount? Easily. We didn't know we were doing it. Because that huge interest payment was buried in the price of everything we bought. We mistakenly called it inflation—that huge, hidden interest payment we made which was hidden in the higher prices for goods and services. Since interest is a cost of business, this cost is passed down the line in high prices.

THIRTY CENTS ON EACH DOLLAR

We can calculate the relative size of this debt another way: by the fourth quarter of 1986 the disposable personal income in current dollars of all Americans was $3 trillion; in 1982 dollars it was $2.6 trillion. Of the assumed $1.1 trillion in interest, much was paid out of our disposable personal income. This means that out of every dollar we spent as consumers, about thirty cents went to pay interest on our collective debts.

Interest compounds. If we paid $800 billion in 1986, we will pay more in 1987, still more in 1988, and so on, with no end of this horrendous debt yet in sight.

As Senator Patrick Moynihan put it in 1984, "Interest rate payments represented the largest transfer of wealth in history from wages to capital."[4] But not many of us knew this was going on. How were we to know? After all, it was hidden in the prices we paid, and hidden in other ways too. It seemed to be hidden even from writers on the subject. In September 1984, the *New York Times* ran an article entitled "If

Inflation Is Licked, How Come String Beans Cost So Much?" This article referred to the price-rise problem; unhappily, it did not explain it.

Similar ignorance has generated many such comments on the economy in the clear belief that the facts presented were important, or at least relevant, but without a firm grasp of how they are relevant and important. So the crisis has grown.

CONTROL

One of our favorite economic ideas of late has been that the federal monetary policy (increasing or decreasing the money supply) and/or fiscal policy (federal deficits and tax adjustments) control the direction of business activity. In other words, U.S. government policy controls the direction of business activity in our $4.2 trillion domestic economy at the end of 1986, which is closely linked to other national economies the world over—which altogether carry, some estimate, over $15 trillion in debts. This model has the U.S. government tail wagging the international economic dog.

Obviously, it was at best just a theoretical or academic notion, this belief that federal authorities could fine-tune the economy by manipulating the appropriate money supply, taxes and government-spending tools. And not everyone bought this notion.

"However," according to former Federal Reserve economist, John Maken, in his book *The Global Debt Crisis*, "money demand, which is subject to random and operationally unpredictable chance, make these adjustments chancy at best . . . the results can be disastrous."[5]

DEBTS

The central economic problem in our society is debt, including its interest. Debt in all four sectors: consumer, corporate, municipal and federal. During the past twenty years, many words have been thrown at federal debt and federal budget deficits, but hardly a mention has been made of debts and deficits in the private sector. This was strange because the total domestic debt load of $11.06 trillion was split about equally among the four sectors.

The federal debt actually totaled about 21%, with the remaining 79% split among consumers, corporations and state/local governments. That 79% is the really dangerous debt, which will—if it hasn't already—upset our apple cart. And that's why I maintain that our economy is in crisis whether or not the big crash has happened by the time you read this.

How sad that this fact will hit us between the eyes only after financial doomsday.

Pyramids

Worse yet, much of this debt was incurred for purposes which were unproductive. It's one thing to take on new debt in order to increase production and therefore be better able to repay. But what we've been building with our collective debt are pyramids. Military waste,

Jacuzzis, motor homes, unneeded new city halls and so on—none of it generating income to liquidate the debt that brought it. The function of this nonproductive wealth has been to build pyramids. Instead of income, our collective debt, with its eternal compound interest load, simply generated more debt.

HISTORY'S LESSON

What has happened in America—this pyramiding of debt—has occurred many times before in world economic history, which is why I find it so unfortunate that we no longer teach economic history in our universities. Instead, we have econometrics and other math-based policies, which have guided short-view economic theories, none of which have worked. If these newly hatched theories had just included debt and compound interest, we might not now have the crisis we have.

History tells us that the future casts its shadow. It was not difficult to see that an economy based on an upside-down pyramid of debt was terminal. But no one with influence believed this. Instead, all solutions for continued growth centered around incurring more and more debt, as witnessed by our successively larger annual federal deficits.

DEBT IS MONEY . . . ?

We all used debt as money. Not consciously, of course. We typically thought of debt as borrowed currency and coin, or additional usable checks. However, a mere 5% of what we call and use as money was coins and currency. Ninety-five percent was debt.

Ah, but we didn't like to call it debt. We called it borrowing, or getting a loan, or bank credit. The automatic loan you get through the check-guarantee provision on your checking account rarely comes as cash. Instead you write checks against that legal overdraft in order to pay bills. Meanwhile, even most experts lost sight of the fact that little is purchased with cash, and much is purchased with checks and other forms of credit. Thus we have kept our economic wheels turning.

Debt became a way of life. We didn't take the federal deficits so seriously—we were used to running up our own debts, everyone was doing it. And all this credit seemed painless enough. Like our checking account overdraft. Future income would cover it.

The monthly payments we made paid little more than the interest, usually. Rarely did we reckon the cost of the cumulative interest, we just paid and paid, and stretched it out as though waiting for a rich aunt to die and bail us out of debt.

That's how debt became big business. Everybody just took it for granted. By 1987 the federal government's debt had grown to $2.37 trillion. That same year we as consumers had borrowed $2.3 trillion on mortgages and in-stallment credit; almost owing as much as Uncle Sam, but no one told the public. Instead, the focus was on federal obigations. Strange.

Tail Wags Dog

The growth of debt led to the growth of "finance." Our present gargantuan financial structures wouldn't exist but for the borrowing mania.

Our financial sector, measured in dollars, is about three times larger than our industrial sector. We watched the proliferation of financial services without considering its root cause. Seemingly on every corner grew banks, brokerage firms, insurance companies, savings & loans, and investment advisors. Instead of making and marketing goods to the world's consumers, we put our wealth and brains into the business of nurturing "finance."

Economic Forecasting Fails

If you have wondered why, since World War II, our economists have done such a bad job of forecasting turns in the economy, you're not alone. *Time* magazine in August 1984 had this to say about the fraternity of economic seers:

"Almost with one voice, the experts a year ago predicted moderate growth and a rise in inflation in 1984. They were spectacularly wrong. Other forecasts have rarely been better. This kind of question is raising serious concerns about the degree to which companies and governments should pay attention to economists at all. The stress in mathematics, which makes a large part of economics incomprehensible to laymen, is a relatively modern development. Adam Smith, David Ricardo and other founding fathers of economics were far more concerned with broad social and political issues than with numerical precisions."[6]

By December 1984 the economic forecasting record continued sour, "missing the mark." This has continued through 1985, 1986 and 1987, concurrent with falling prices.

The *Wall Street Journal* reported in July 1984 that commodity prices had fallen 24% since the previous year. More important, 14% of that drop had occurred since May of that same year.[7]

The World Bank in its *World Development Report* 1987 reported that in 1985 the World Bank's index of 33 non-fuel primary commodity prices, in current dollar terms, fell to its lowest level in nine years. For the first time in recent history, practically all commodity groups experienced price declines in the first half of 1984. Clearly, something new and dramatic and terrible was going on since accumulated commodities represented wealth which was silently vanishing in falling prices.

All the while, this intensifying decline in prices (which is deflation) was generally ignored. Consumers actually saw the prices of the things they were buying at retail rising even by early 1988. But, and this is important, this was due to the interest cost on the total debt load. Interest is a cost and it is added back into prices, so prices rose—soft drinks were fifty cents a can, for example. The public saw this as inflation when the reality was the silent interest burden we all paid every time we spent a dime. (I will explore this phenomena further in subsequent chapters.) But don't blame the public for seeing inflation—that's what they were told by the experts, who apparently did not understand this historical event either.

If there had been enough people around who remembered 1928 and 1929 and the rapid disintegration of prices then, we might have had a panic in 1984 because of this dramatic decline in commodity prices. But our modern public has been on a twenty-five year binge and has grown complacent. We no longer look behind the scenes, ask hard questions or think very deeply. Few alive now have a personal, vivid memory of hard times in the 1930s. So the fact that a sharp and swift decline has happened only three times in our century had little impact. It was, however, a signal announcing the coming crisis.

LIFE OF ITS OWN

Bad mathematical economic forecasting has taken on a life of its own. Year after year it fails, and year after year economists are sought to make still more bad forecasts. Someone, on the event of the Great Depression, said, "Prosperity is just around the corner." Whoever said that—it probably wasn't Herbert Hoover, after all—could probably still find a job today as an economic forecaster. Economic output plunged 2.5% in 1982, in one of the severest recessions since the end of World War II. Not one of the economists had predicted a recession.

"In automobiles, they can recall their mistakes. We can't recall,"[8] stated Bob Eggert of Sedona, Arizona, who surveyed the economists for his monthly *Blue Chip Economic* indicators. In a remarkable exercise of humility, Eggert calculated the Blue Chip's record of accuracy over 10 years and found it missed the GNP growth by an average of one percentage point each year. In today's economy, that kind of error amounts to either missing or overstating $38 billion worth of economic output—dishwashers, legal services, computer chips, cosmetics. So what good are economists? Some people are beginning to ask that question.

The history of very long economic cycles, or any business cycle for that matter, are ignored by the mass of Ph.D. economists. The reason is obvious: if there is anything to cycles, those in nature being replicated in business, for example, then economic theory and practice has little validity; the cycles will happen regardless of what economists think will happen. Also, as far back as 1955, mainstream economists led by W.W. Rostow developed new economic theories that suggested everlasting growth and the concomitant banishment of Depressions. This defied the long history of industrial capitalism, but it was still economic gospel, and for many economists it still is.

Historically, for better or for worse, that is the way the world seems to work. Maybe economists should be more contrite and recognize economics as an art form instead of a science!

In 1969 the Nobel Prize for Economic Science was established (funded by the Central Bank of Sweden, not by the Nobel legacy). That event finally allowed economists to take their place beside the physicists, chemists and biologists. A Swedish professor, Erick Lundberg, justified this award by noting that "economic science has developed increasingly in the direction of a mathematical specification and statistical quantification of economic contexts. This has proven successful and has left far behind the vague, more literary type of economics with which most laymen are familiar."

In endorsing the economists, the Nobel Committee was doing no more than endorsing the conception of economics that politicians in government and business leaders have acted on since World War II. This had led to the President's Economic Council and to economists becoming an indispensable part of the industrial state's panoply of expertise.

I am sorry that my historical economic background is no longer a part of the dominant style. And I am aware, of course, that mainstream economists work overtime to defend their theoretical territorial turf. To me, economics has been a lot more of an art form than a science. Therefore, to question theoretical givens, such as the widely held belief that the Federal Reserve controls the money supply and other dogmas so widely trusted and believed is to invite wrath from the ivory tower on down.

ARE "EXPERTS" BLIND?

Billions of dollars worth of daily transactions in many currencies compose the life of the world economy today. Most of these transactions involve credit to one or both parties involved. Out of these loans has grown the $15-plus trillion (by 1987) in world debt. And this debt is a dead load on the world economy. Even payments on interest and principle were being recycled to further debt. So much is being spent to serve old debt that spending on new goods is reduced.

Of course, that reduced spending feeds back into the world economy as reduced demand. Falling demand causes falling prices for the world's products and this overall decline is accelerating.

While all this was happening, policymakers the world over were not noticing it. Historically, these people are like generals who are fighting the last war. Blind policymakers are still fighting inflation, over which they are powerless anyway. This makes little difference because, given the magnitude of the debt problem, they think and act as though they *do* have power over the economy.

Until the final collapse, their posturing is about all we have to watch. But we shouldn't blame them; we all ignored the lessons of history.

DEBT CAUSES FALLING PRICES

Controlled credit turns the wheels of industry. Runaway credit builds a debt and interest burden too big for the turning wheels to pay back. This dead burden raising the price of finished goods finally reduces demand for goods and, in turn, demand for feedstocks from which goods are made. When demand for commodities fall, so do their prices. Falling prices of commodities and goods equals shrinking economic activity and money supply (largely credit). At some point, the downward spiral can't be reversed and no amount of new credit pumped in by the Fed makes any difference.

The increasing scarcity of money (because people aren't creating it by taking the credit offered) finally means the interest price of money will escalate. We then witness a surplus of goods and a scarcity of money.

Financial panic is the result of this closed cycle of economic events after they reach the uncontrollable stage. It has happened in America with astonishing regularity. Since 1800 it has occurred eight times, including 1929. And now we are looking at number nine!

CHAPTER 1

EXTRAORDINARY POPULAR DELUSIONS AND THE MADNESS OF CROWDS

Price Rise Delusion

This chapter bears the title of a book written by Charles Mackay in 1841. Mass delusions are not rare. They salt the human story. The reason? As historian Edmund Schiller wrote, "Anyone taken as an individual is tolerably sensible and reasonable—as a member of a crowd, he at once becomes a blockhead."[1]

Mackay detailed the great delusions which captured the imagination of millions of people simultaneously: Tulipmania, the Mississippi Scheme, the South Sea Bubble, the Crusades and witch hunts, to name a few.

As I write this book, Americans suffer a number of economic delusions: their bank deposits are safe; the government can and will prevent another depression; the Fed controls our economy; the government occasionally prints too much money; all money is green paper or silver coin; and in any worst-case scenario government emergency programs will prevent hardship and death. But the greatest of all popular delusions extant is that inflation is permanent.

Complicating that last delusion, here before the crash, was the still-perpetuated definition of inflation as a rise in prices. Prices have no place in the definition. Inflation is the unwarranted increase in the money supply. Prices usually, but not always, rise as a result of inflating the money supply.

Money supply inflation (or debt inflation, since money is 95% credit) actually has accelerated since the 1930s. The public had no reason to note this until the 1970s, when prices suddenly rose dramatically. During the following ten years it became easy to think that inflation (read: price rises) would continue forever. It was also easy to buy the definition. Hence price rises became inflation. The concept of permanent inflation (with or without its usual impact on prices) proved to be a dangerous idea. Inflation, a wealth of current data now confirms, ended in 1979. Key prices fell from then until the crash, which I am assuming will have happened by the time most of you read this. Because those key prices were in commodities, we as consumers were not aware that inflation had ended. We saw gasoline prices go down (a little) but no major cuts. Thus we were inclined to believe that prices would rise forever.

One final fact of our fundamental pre-crash delusion: most people did relate the price rises to money supply correctly (though they lumped both phenomena under inflation). But they erred in seeing the cause of inflation as the government printing too much paper money. Well, the government was the culprit for that—and for running budgets so much bigger than its income from taxes could support. But few understood that we used credit as a substitute for money, and that the root cause of our recent inflation was the extraordinary explosion of bank credit in the private sector.

It is not the government's budget that is the culprit, since out of $11 trillion in debt (that is, credits we have used) only $2.3 trillion, or 21%, is government debt. The other 79% of our real collective debt lies with consumers, corporations, cities and states. The credit expansion of all sectors was much faster than the output of goods and services, and this was reflected in rapid price rises during the 1970s. So much for the cause.

Thus, before the crash, we had not only the great delusion itself but all of its relatives to keep we citizen/consumer/taxpayers from seeing reality. For the reality is that this expected permanent inflation is rapidly dying. Already in many sections of the country, the home owner's notion that the value of his home will do nothing but increase has fallen prey to the reality of falling real estate values. And this has undermined the cherished belief that it's the American way for things to get better instead of worse.

Nor is education any guarantee against the malady of such delusions and myths, especially for those who have been educated beyond their capacity to use their common sense.

Soon to be gone, if it isn't already, is the false confidence that the government or Federal

Reserve can control the economy or prevent catastrophe. And catastrophe is the proper word, for this is no trivial event. Both financially and psychologically, it means the end of an era, the end of optimism and good times and the beginning of pessimism and hard times, of muddling through and just getting along.

Could the government have forestalled this? No. But the government can and now must intervene in ways used often in the past, such as:

1. Limiting withdrawals from banks to minimal sums, when the time comes, thus stemming bank runs. This should last until the public calms down and is willing to again accept credit checks.

2. Closing all banks, as happened in March of 1933, then reopen those few which are liquid and solvent. Nationalize all remaining banks, severely limiting the ability to produce another credit monster.

3. Declaring to foreign holders of U.S. government IOUs that we cannot buy them back. Freezing foreign deposits in U.S. banks, and preventing American citizens from transferring their foreign assets home in dollars, or visiting their assets abroad.

4. Declaring a housing moratorium (delaying payments due), a period when loans and payments are frozen until the prices of

homes can be written down to real world values. In some cases, this will mean a decline of up to 80% from today's "asking" prices.

As in all previous mass delusions, the public is the last to learn that the bubble has burst. Now it is hardly important to realize that inflation has been over for a long time; it is now quite important to know that prices will fall and will continue to fall for many years to come. Deflation follows inflation as night follows day. "Growth" will become a memory. Staying alive will become the new economic reality.

Think About This

Looking back from 1988 it seems the economic world that exploded from 1945 to the early 1980s is now passing into history much as the Roman Empire did. It cannot be made to work again despite faith (which now seems to be blind faith) in the old order.

The old economic system—burdened with its old economic theories—has changed too much now to get it in high gear again. For example:

In the early days of our economic system, borrowing to start a new business was rewarded with gains that repaid the borrowed funds. The economy experienced real growth and was debt free because of this ongoing process. Now all economic growth is negative because it must be financed by ever larger deficits at home and abroad which will never be repaid. This is neither good nor positive. It is bad news.

Even gigantic military spending has lost its power to stimulate the economy as it once did. Proof of this is seen in the ever larger deficits which are needed to do the same job as before.

CHAPTER 2

A NEW ATTITUDE

On August 15, 1971, President Nixon closed the gold window. This meant the U.S. dollar could no longer be exchanged for its equivalent sum in gold. It was a break with the past, as England had done two generations earlier.

Think Inflation

The final severance of our dollar's link to gold in 1971 created among Americans a new attitude, one previously unknown in our history. There had been in our past short periods (e.g., during wartime) when an inflationary psychology held sway. But it had never persisted for an indefinite time, and had never been as all-pervasive as it has become between 1971 and the inevitable crash.

This inflationary psychology naturally resulted in the government being viewed with less confidence. Life in general appeared different. The spirit of cooperation with government vanished and it was viewed with pessimism. Scheming, speculation and sophisticated tax avoidance tended to replace, or at least color, productive effort, saving and long-range planning.

Speculative activities blossomed. Trading in currencies became more rewarding to banks than the traditional business of brokering loans from savings. The futures and options market turned into giant gambling games. The new markets that developed after the dollar lost its precise value definition in gold reflect the limitless ingenuity of mankind. We saw futures sold in currencies, and betting on the monetary inflation of various governments. Instead of buying a bond or treasury bill and holding it, we began high-volume speculation on a daily basis.

In the fall of 1982 the trading of futures and options on stock market indexes began. It became possible to buy futures on large certificates of deposit as well. Outstanding European rate futures were offered, and starting in 1975, GNMA options came on line. Billions of dollars were packaged in business and industry for takeover attempts, both successful and otherwise. Such piracy games became popular, wasteful and frightening, completely ignoring the real needs of new industries and the recapitalization of old. The total amount devoted to these speculative ventures came to trillions of dollars. And all these new, unproductive games of chance had their origins in unsound money.

With a sound currency there would be no speculation and trading in U.S. government bonds, notes and bills—or it would be minimal, because the value of government IOUs would be predictable, so betting on their day-to-day fluctuations in value would be meaningless. By 1980 on the Chicago Board of Trade, far more U.S. Treasury bond futures contracts were traded than cattle contracts.

The options market grew by leaps and bounds, becoming more sophisticated and complex every day. The frenzy with which this speculation mushroomed was beyond measure—and literally incomprehensible, irrational. Frenzy is the proper word. And it was destined to end in economic collapse.

This spirit of speculation by 1980 had spread to the fiscal arena. State-run lotteries collected $2,107,325,000 that year. It was illegal for most citizens to gamble in most states, but it was legal for governments to operate lotteries in order to raise revenues.

M1, M1+, M2, M3 . . . ?

Since 1971 the definition of money has undergone a continuous change, reflecting the new rules of our fiat monetary system. In 1970 there was *one* way of counting the money supply (they call this a monetary aggregate). In 1971 the concepts of M1, M2 and M3 were introduced. By 1975 it became necessary to define two new aggregates: M4 and M5. As money management became increasingly uncertain after the money-gold divorce, the definition of money had to undergo continuous change. After the mid-1970s, demand deposits were virtually impossible to calculate because of the new interest-bearing transaction (checking) accounts. That brought in 1978 the temporary use of a measurement called M1 +.

After the turbulent international monetary crisis of 1979, many were convinced that current definitions and money management were totally inadequate, so all monetary aggregates had to be redefined again. Four definitions were introduced (adding to the old definitions): M1-A, M1-B, M3, M2.

This problem of measuring monetary aggregates would not exist under a gold standard, needless to say, since there would be no purpose to it.

The American Dream

During the years just prior to the collapse of the late 1980s, Americans became aware that their national dream was less certain, if not fast fading. Their gut feeling told them the American standard of living was more likely to go down than up. Many Americans recognized, at least dimly, that inflation and the tax code were transferring wealth from the large middle class and working poor to the rich and welfare poor. People knew that the IRS 1040 deduction for dependents was not keeping pace with inflation. They saw that an average income could no longer buy a house. Cars were smaller for the shrinking number able to afford them, and drivers began pumping their own gas. Household help and other personalized services were on the wane. And out of this came a ferment of negativity, a chronic sense of frustration and anger, even hopelessness—that maybe "we are the last generation."

A growing number of Americans resorted to the underground economy to compensate for losses they saw as unfair. As during prohibition, we rationalized our petty (and not so petty) lawbreaking: drugs, cheating on taxes, Wall Street "insider" trading, etc. This uncertainty and fear of loss created a new subculture of financial survivalists, who were convinced by their own analysis that the government would not adopt a sound and equitable monetary system.

This subculture no longer depended on conventional news services for their information, but came to rely on expensive newsletters for what they judged to be accurate information on monetary affairs. It was easy to dismiss this subculture as speculators, but their existence was really a statement on U.S. monetary policy, for they were refusing to lose 5% a year to inflation by owning "secure" government bonds.

Other Americans faced with inflation attempted to preserve long-term assets. During the past fifteen years thousands have attended hard-money conferences in the hope of learning how to protect themselves when the government would not. Prior to 1974 hard-money survivalists conferences were virtually unheard of. It was a new phenomenon, and is directly related to the breakdown of the Bretton Woods and Smithsonian Agreements.

When Nixon removed the control of gold from

the U.S. credit dollar in 1971, because we could not honor gold claims anymore, there was simply too much credit outstanding. This set the stage for the bank credit binge and borrowing, which the U.S. embarked on, and which set another stage for the 1970s inflation: the vast increase in bank-credit dollars.

Gold Bugs

Hard-money conferences took hold when the public saw gold rise to $850 an ounce in 1980. The hard-money people believed then, and still believe, the rise in gold was caused by the government printing too much paper money, and gold rose as paper money devalued in worth. They perceived then, and still believe they see, that inflation reviving and accelerating yet another hyper-inflation. Along the way they forgot that in all of recorded history, what follows inflation is deflation, not more inflation. Raw material prices started to fall in 1974, and this fall accelerated in 1980. There has never before been an inflation preceded by falling commodity prices—not in all of history. But so much for the lessons of history. The hard-money people are hard believers in the verity of gold. So much for that now moribund idea.

Among their numbers were a vocal minority which desired the abandonment of gold convertability and predicted the subsequent events of the late 1970s.

Throughout the prolonged dissolution of the

gold standard (1913 to 1971) there remained a remnant steadfastly convinced that one day gold would be needed to stop inflation, to restore order in monetary policy, and to stabilize financial markets. Their number increased rapidly, but not rapidly enough, as events during the 1980s have dramatized. Certainly there is a need to establish a modern guarantee for currency, if credit itself is not to be controlled and manipulated. But return to the gold standard, as conservative economists and politicians have preached, is hardly likely now that the computer and telex have welded the world into one economic unit. A world gold standard is possible, of course, but not probable.

No Return to a Gold Standard

One way to force a country to live within its means (defined by the amount of gold it owns) is to adopt a gold standard. The argument goes that the only way to inflating the currency then would be to repeal the legislation that established a gold standard to begin with. The believers in a gold standard live in a happy delusion that inflation is history and people can go about their lives with no worry. It's a fool's paradise. The full benefit of a gold standard can only be obtained when a nation is in control of its currency—but nations are not in control of their currencies. The score of new financial instruments (repurchase agreements) amount to a private issue of currency and these, in the aggregate, distort national monetary policy. The experts forget that cheap money has always been far more attractive than dear money. Privately issued financial instruments are cheaper and far more plentiful than gold-backed money, which is finite.

When the economy begins to expand, bankers will find a way to expand credit to keep pace, and sooner or later (Gresham's Law) the newly invented financial instruments (cheaper money) will drive out dearer money. Bank-issued, or private sector-issued, cheap money amounts to an inflation of the currency, however much the public believed in the 1980s that the federal government caused this to happen.

In a gold-standard country, privately issued funds are also redeemable in gold. When cashed in for gold, it draws down the supply of gold, causing deflation, and this can only be replenished if the government makes new purchases of gold. It's either that, or let credit vanish. And the consequences of vanishing credit amount to financial doomsday.

Nothing is solved by a gold standard: control of the money supply is lost, not gained, and the government is left with the choice of (1) buying more gold, or (2) creating massive deflation. A return to the gold standard would take us back to square one, but worse off. We forget history: the last time gold ruled the economy, depressions were the order of the day. But now the existence of the private currencies adds a frightening new dimension, which is why we are now on the brink of Great Depression II: the vast bank credit, especially the private credit expansion of $8.68 trillion during the past fifteen years, will end with a nightmarish credit collapse. And we will relearn the ancient lesson that debt is debt, now as it was in the beginning. It wasn't debt that changed during recent decades, it was our perception of it, as we wallowed in easy credit.

The Powerful Forces of Deflation

In the middle 1970s we experienced a powerful inflation. And suddenly, it seemed, everyone knew all about inflation.

Then the rising curve was reversed. But few people noticed the change. It was subtle. As late as 1987 policymakers were still warning against inflation. Alas.

What is deflation? Inflation upside-down. Falling prices for everything. Smaller salaries, lower rents, lower real estate prices. Lower prices for cars, VCRs, foods. The disappearances of luxury goods, winter vacations, foreign travel.

It's also soaring unemployment, riots in the streets, more and more people going broke, banks going bust, savings & loans for sale, and a growing feeling of dismay, public arousal. Most of all it is fear.

Fear is a more powerful emotion than greed. The growth of our American wealth has been propelled by various stages of greed and fear.

By the time the scandals of 1986 greed had risen, the tide had changed.

Will and Ariel Durant wrote in *The Lessons of History* a summary of their twenty-volume history of civilization, "History repeats itself in the large because human nature changes with gradual leisureliness, and man is equipped to respond in stereotyped ways to frequently occurring situations, and stimulants like hunger, danger, sex."[1]

In other words, human nature is predictable. It does not change very much. You may think you are different from your parents. Not likely. You'll act very much like people did in all past depressions: scared.

Our contemporary delusion did not originate yesterday, as you can see by the price and real wage charts on the following page.

Notice that prices fall relentlessly. Every uptick during this period was hailed by our experts and our media as proof that the worm had turned. But the problem was far deeper than the habitat of worms. And this fact was first discovered, to my knowledge, by the French historian Fernand Braudel, who wrote:

"The longest lasting of all these [economic] cycles is the secular trend, and it is perhaps the most neglected. Barely visible in real life, but plodding inexorably on, always in the same direction, this trend is a cumulative process, building on its own achievements, almost as if it were determined gradually to raise the mass of prices and economic activities until some turning point, when, with equal obstinancy, it begins working to bring them down again, slowly and imperceptibly but over a long period. Year by year it is hardly discernible, but measured century by century it is something of importance. Four successive secular cycles can be identified: 1250-1507, 1507-1733, 1733-1817, and 1817-1974. With evidence of only three secular cycles— the fourth, if we are right, about 1974 as being a turning point [the chart indicates it was]—we can draw conclusions about the comparative length of these cycles:

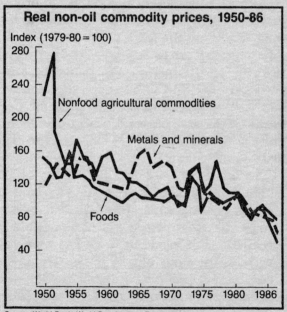

Real non-oil commodity prices, 1950-86

Index (1979-80 = 100)

Nonfood agricultural commodities

Metals and minerals

Foods

Source: World Bank, World Development Report 1987

Two Faces of Inflations:

1) Nominal

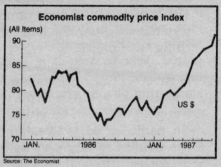

Economist commodity price Index
(All Items)

90
85
80
75
70

JAN.   1986   JAN.   1987

US $

Source: The Economist

2) Real

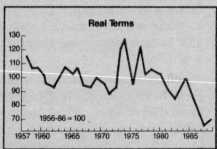

Real Terms

130
120
110
100
90
80
70

1956-86 = 100

1957 1960 1965 1970 1975 1980 1985

Source: IMF, World Economic Outlook, April 1987
Data after end-1986 are estimates

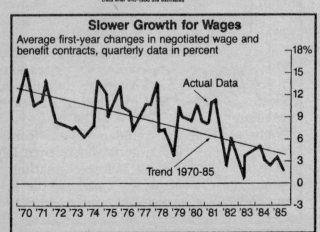

Slower Growth for Wages

Average first-year changes in negotiated wage and
benefit contracts, quarterly data in percent

18%
15
12
9
6
3
0
-3

Actual Data

Trend 1970-85

'70 '71 '72 '73 '74 '75 '76 '77 '78 '79 '80 '81 '82 '83 '84 '85

Source: Bureau of Labor Statistics

around 125 years. The peaks of 1350, 1650, 1817, and 1973-74 were vantage points and watersheds. After the longest cycles, everything is changed."[2]

Most economic experts saw this long cycle not as 125 years but in terms of the Kondratieff wave cycle of about 50 years. The Kondratieff cycle, named after its Russian discoverer, came to be written in stone to its believers. If they were correct, it could be a most useful tool for predicting. But it could not.

THE DEFLATIONARY TRAP

Deflation brings in its wake problems that seem beyond solution. During the years of the Great Depression debts declined 20%. But the value of underlying assets (including real estate) and the price of goods declined 75%. So after the first four years of the Great Depression, debt had not been reduced. It had actually increased by 40% or more.

Faced with $212 billion in debt, falling land prices and falling farm commodity prices, our farmers could not produce enough cash flow to repay the debt they had incurred when prices were high.

Credit is based on confidence. Once confidence is gone, credit is gone. There then follows bankruptcies, bank failures, creating a scramble for liquid dollar assets. By the autumn of 1987, this series of events had yet to materialize. But the trend had been set in motion.

When price declines begin to be noticed, they are labeled by the media as "disinflation." That's part of the delusion. It's deflation, not disinflation. What made this deflation worse in our time is that the real wages of the average American worker had also been falling since 1973. The roots of the problem were deep.

Unlike rising prices, falling prices hurt people and businesses whose incomes are tied to prices. What they buy today is worth less tomorrow. The grocer or the gas station owner pay less for their products and so can sell them for less.

However, in the real world, such merchants accumulate inventories of their goods—to assure regular supply and to protect themselves against rising prices. The next thing they know, the prices of their inventories have fallen and they are forced to sell for less.

For individuals or businesses with little debt and fixed or rising incomes, deflation is a boon—until that is, it pulls down the whole economy. Deflation was at the core of the Great Depression, history tells us, and then as now when deflation gathers force, businessmen can no longer make prices by passing on their rising debt costs and interest burdens to consumers. They must take losses.

HISTORY REPEATS

During the Great Depression, Marriner Eccles, Chairman of the Federal Reserve Board, wrote in 1933:

"The supply of money tends to contract when the rate of spending declines. Thus, during the depression, the money, instead of expanding to moderate the effect of decreased rates of spending contracted, and soon intensified the depression."[3]

Where were rates of spending declining in 1986 and 1987?

1. The continued fall in prices clearly showed that less spending was going on since it takes less credit money to buy things when prices are low than when they are high.

2. The real wages of workers have been falling since 1973. They have less to spend; therefore they spend less.

3. Continued bank and S&L failures curtailed spending.

4. Perhaps most important, the spending that was going on during the middle 1980s was losing its impact since much of it was used to repay old debts and pay interest. So $100 "spent" shrank to maybe less than $50 left to turn the wheels of commerce. As an example of this staggering process, the Federal Reserve Bank of New York in the summer of 1986 reported that the average American was spending 74% of each $1 of disposable personal income to pay his mortgage and installment debts. This left him

with 26 cents of real spending. Obviously, this was too much non-productive spending, not productive since it did not generate wealth.

In theory, credit is fine if used to make something productive, something that will produce an income with which to repay the debt. But if it only produces interest for someone else, it is not productive.

Thus, the decline in the rate of spending continued to shrink the money supply and contract credit.

WHAT IS CONTRACTING CREDIT?

Before a financial panic there is less credit. How does less credit originate? When the price of oil was $29 a barrel, it took a lot of bank credit to finance it, but when the price fell to $15, it took less credit. So credit contracted. Later, this was seen in reduced spending by the major oil companies for other things, like public broadcasting, gifts to the Girl Scouts, etc.

This contraction spread like a plague, but it was ignored. Too many experts were waiting for the final evidence: debts going into liquidation because reduced cash flows made it impossible to pay them. But the contracting credit process had begun long before.

My experience is that most people simply do not comprehend this. Certainly most economists don't; they're too busy counting growth and credit expansion, mistakenly believing that these originate at the Federal Reserve. So they did not add up the colossal credit contraction America was undergoing all during the 1980s. Old thinking habits die hard.

CHAPTER 3

THE HISTORIC ECONOMIC PENDULUM

On average, fundamental economic change is completed in about one generation. These crucial changes may be compared to a pendulum swinging back and forth, always seeking equilibrium. In the early 1980s, for example, we were overwhelmed with old and new credit extensions at every level. The credit collapse would come when the swinging pendulum reached its outer limit, where such credit extensions are self-correcting in forced liquidation.

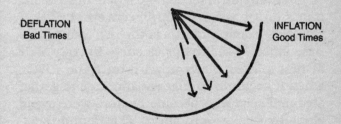

DEFLATION
Bad Times

INFLATION
Good Times

Once the pendulum starts to swing, nothing can prevent its course from being completed.

Why do most of us not see the inevitability of this at the time? Largely because economists, generally, are like the rest of us: they seek order and predictability, the status quo. They are generally uniformists (smooth slope) types, who deride or ignore their opposite school with its catastrophic (fits and jerks) view of economic history. Big changes disturb the status quo, which is a great discomfort to economists and other uniformists.

Because of this preference for order, most of us are rudely jarred by spectacular economic events, while ignoring their earlier and not-so-obvious root causes. But it is major historic change, not order, which often explains why some people make fortunes and others lose them. During favorable long-term trends many people "fall into money." They really don't know how it all happened, but of course like to attribute their new wealth to innate shrewdness, to their hard and dedicated labor, or to their provident father in heaven. In most cases, however, the money machine—with its origins outside their ken—carried them along on its unperceived, powerful conveyer belt.

A vivid example of this is the real estate business since 1946. The price curve in real estate at first started slowly upward until the 1970s, when it began to strengthen and then to gather steam. Those who became realtors were swept along by this upward curve. They found themselves in a business where price rises followed inflation and made them money. People in real estate profited by just being alive. The impending crash, now gathering momentum, will be especially painful for them. Most didn't even know they'd been on a free ride, much less why.

The Long-Term Decline in Liquidity

This is major trend number one. The most important, basic pre-crash change was the precipitous decline in liquidity, caused by growing debt, in all sectors of the U.S. economy. From the end of World War II, when we were the most liquid nation in the world, we have become the most illiquid.

By the mid-1980s we had come dangerously close to a condition wherein the state would become the ultimate creditor. Every day a free enterprise business looked to the government for financial aid: Continental Illinois Bank, savings & loans and small banks by the score; farmers, oilmen and, by late 1987, major stock brokerage firms were at the door of the Fed asking for help (they owed the banks and the banks needed credit).

So the Fed did all it could do and that was to add reserves to the banking system, but reserves are not credit. And what the brokerage firms needed were new loans (credit) to bail out their estimated $1.5 billion in losses which occurred when the stock market crashed on October 19, 1987.

The Fed created, through the *private bank-*

ing system, more debt on this small scale. Could the Fed create $100 billion to save banks with bad Latin loans? Hardly. The total assets of the Federal Reserve system amount to about $250 billion in U.S. Treasury securities. In fact, if you combine the Bank of America and Citibank in New York, their assets were larger than the vaunted Federal Reserve.

Credit is the other side of the debt coin. The following data from 1985 shows $5.8 trillion in Federal debt—which is not all there was by their count. Note also that 20% is federal debt, but 80% is private. While our collective attention was focused on the former as being the big problem, it was, all along, the instability of private debt that threatened.

Outstanding Debt
(Indexes: 1965 = 100)

Borrower	1965	1970	1975	1980	1985
Government(a)	100	123.1	182.4	284.5	585.8
Consumers(b)	100	140.1	226.8	421.2	696.5
Nonfinancial business	100	165.2	277.9	468.8	762.3
Financial business	100	200.5	421.6	917.0	1920.2
TOTAL	100	144.6	236.5	414.4	742.4

(a) Includes federal, state and local governments

(b) This category is called "households" in the source of these statistics. Although consumers are the overwhelming component, the data also include personal trusts, nonprofit foundations, private schools and hospitals, labor unions and churches.

Source: Federal Reserve Board, *Monthly Review,* October 1986

Domestic debt totals in the U.S. are even more startingly revealed by using dollar totals instead of Index Numbers, as follows:

Total Domestic U.S. Debt in 1982 Dollars*

(All numbers in trillions)

	TOTAL		% of Total
Gross Federal Debt (1987)	$2.37	$2.37	21%
City & State Debt (Sept. 1986)	$1.55	$1.55	
Corporate Debt (3rd Qtr. 1986)	$2.81	$2.81	79%
Financial Business (Dec. 1986)	$2.0	$2.01	
Consumer Debts:			
Mortgage Debt (1987)	$1.590		
Installment Credit (Dec. 1986)	$ .739		
Total Consumer	$2.329	$2.32	
1987 GRAND TOTAL DEBT U.S.		$11.06	100%

*The totals for 1988 are all larger. Compound interest, discussed "plows on Sunday" and makes the numbers larger.

Source: *Economic Report of the President 1987*

It is interesting that although much attention is paid by the media and the other financial experts to the huge Federal debts, rarely do either of those sources note that private sector debts are much larger and far more dangerous than TNT. This is because of their bad historical debt repayment record.

The consumer debt is always the weakest link since most consumers have no direct control over their income. They often work for a corporation which lets them go—out of the blue—and this means their debts will go unpaid. Two family incomes are leveraged to that level, so one fallen income, the party is over for a family and they approach bankruptcy quickly.

Municipalities have a miserable debt repayment record. According to a study made by the Twentieth Century Fund in 1938 (*Debts & Recovery*, 20th Century Fund, New York) on changes in the debt structure during 1929 to 1937, "As many as 3,250 American municipalities were in default simultaneously, but that was less than 2% of the 175,000 municipalities in the U.S. back then; there were three states and 310 larger cities with debts totaling $2.22 billion."

Many states back then passed enabling acts which allowed them to write down the interest and the principal they paid, sticking holders to that debt.

If you are among the many sitting on a pile of tax-free municipal debt as you read this, you might consider buying ninety-day Treasury bills instead and pay your taxes to preserve your capital. It is not a wild assumption to state that cities and states are far more precariously poised financially now than they were fifty years ago. Many of them were teetering on bankruptcy by late 1987.

When World War II ended, America was holding most of the world's gold. It had been sent here for safekeeping. And every American seemed to have money. Savings were high and corporations were flush. It was a happy time. Then a long, broad trend started that was to eventually bring us to our knees: we changed from a cash liquid society to a debt-illiquid society.

Now we find ourselves the most debt-ridden society in the history of the world. And after the crash, lenders will be forced to eat their loans through involuntary liquidation. Recorded economic history shows no alternative. The crash will mean—or does mean, if it's happened by the time you read this—massive liquidations on a scale never before seen, and perhaps never to be seen again.

And all of us will witness this unhappy drama, made sadder by the fact that so much of this debt has been nonproductive. We used our borrowed money for consumption rather than production. We spent tomorrow's anticipated income not by increasing our real wealth, but by having a good time.

Years ago, while doing research at the Wharton School, I observed the futility of contracting more and more debt. I was working on a paper titled, "The Profitableness of Borrowed Long-Term Capital." I studied just under five hundred corporations to see how borrowing via bonds fared as compared to generating funds in other ways. Firms issuing bonds soon became inextricably entwined in what can be properly called "a fixed charge debacle." Their steady interest expense continued to eat away at profits and ruined their profitability without fail. The more debt, the less profit.

Note this proof which follows at Sharon Steel after borrowing more, which consumed their earnings.

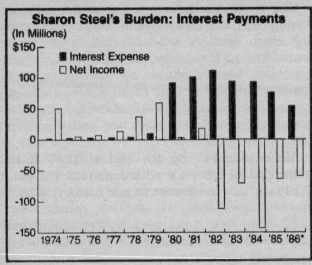

Sharon Steel's Burden: Interest Payments

(In Millions)

- ■ Interest Expense
- □ Net Income

*First 9 months
Source: *Wall Street Journal*, July 14, 1987

BANK LIQUIDITY

A charitable word for the state of our banks is "distressed." Not just for Continental Bank—it was merely the first to go belly-up . . . at a time when the government was yet able to save it by extraordinary means. Continental's distress was merely the first clear indication that the trend was gathering momentum. Others would follow, and did.

Did the banks make too many lenient loans? Did they believe the Fed would always bail them out of trouble? It little matters now, because banks all over the country allowed their capital reserves to decline to what would ordinarily be unthinkable levels for any enterprise . . . except, I suppose, a bank.

In 1904, the first year for which data was computed, the average bank had capital equivalent to total liabilities—a ratio of 100%. As America grew stronger and more stable, this ratio gradually declined. By 1910, three years before the Fed's birth in 1913, the ratio was equivalent to over 21% of liabilities. After 1913 the ratio continued to decline and was 11.5% before World War II. By 1970 the ratio had declined to 8.4%. By the end of 1980 it had dropped to 6.8% for all commercial banks. In 1983 it was the lowest in our history: 4.3%. It is even lower now.

Along with this decline in capital reserve went a decline in cash reserves. At the time the Federal Reserve Act was passed, banks kept cash equal to, on the average, 22% of total assets. This figure was 16% in 1970, 12.5% in 1981, 9% in 1983, and lower now. By then, the volatility of all markets was signaling a panic, and in that climate the quality of bank assets became crucial. But in late 1987, with foreign loans frozen, with bond portfolios down almost 40% and with very low reserves, the banks were sitting ducks.

WHAT THE FED CAN AND CANNOT DO

In the pre-crash liquidity crisis conventional wisdom had the Fed stepping in as the bank of last resort to save the system and give us sleep-filled nights. Of course, the Fed did *not* possess that power, and the pendulum continued its swing. The liquidity crisis became a bomb. A triggering event lit the fuse. Word spread. The resulting chaos saw depositors, large and small, run for their money, making a bad situation impossible.

Let me explain "liquidity crisis." It means a shortage of credit. One thing economists excel in is the misuse of their own language. Thus, the public thinks being liquid is being close to cash, near cash assets. But economists, in their Wizard of Oz world, think of adding liquidity to mean adding new debt.

Therefore, when liquidity contracts, as it does in deflation, we reach the point where there is very little credit available for anyone, except at an extraordinary rate of interest. And that's what is called a liquidity squeeze, or crisis. By late 1987 Mexico was going through this drama with credit being almost impossible to obtain. A rate of 150% a year there was not uncommon. Will we in the U.S. reach that illiquidity benchmark before our current crisis ends? We could.

If the crash hasn't come by the time you read this, realize one thing: the Fed does *not* possess the power to save the banking system. The pendulum swings.

American corporate debt has built-in limits. We might assume, for the sake of argument, that the sale of corporate bonds, mortgaging property and obtaining new bank loans can keep going endlessly. But it can't, not unless businesses can generate the goods and services to make enough profit to meet ever rising interest payments—and that's not what has happened in the 1980s.

Unfortunately, debt from continuous borrowing does not expand in a creeping arithmetic fashion. It accelerates geometrically. It is the interest burden on debt which multiplies as a cancer to choke off profits, erode management incentives and overcome the financial prowess needed to keep profit-making activities growing.

Thus, when this era ends, we will see, with 20-20 hindsight, that the major events in business which disrupted our lives were always financial, not productive. To those with historically tuned foresight, it wasn't difficult to see an incomparable liquidity crisis in the making. Even as we entered 1989, illiquidity (profits not covering expenses) was our greatest domestic threat by far.

Creating Demand by Borrowing

Major trend number two, before the crash, was the failure of capitalist economies to fit the Keynesian theory. This was a profound economic phenomenon. The Keynesian model proclaimed that governments can, by prudent intervention, control economies. Governments, the Keynesians say, by using fiscal means (cutting taxes or spending) and by monetary means (adjusting the money supply), stimulate or curtail growth, and prevent severe recessions and/or depressions. And for a couple of decades after World War II, this Keynesian idea seemed to work. At least we did not suffer any severe recessions.

Mainstream economists were so busy congratulating themselves they barely noticed when, in November 1977, a Japanese official was quoted by the *Wall Street Journal* as saying, "Those fiscal and monetary measures that have worked fifteen years aren't working as they used to."[1] And, indeed, Keynesian methods were not working, for they had stumbled after 1962. Why?

Fiscal and monetary measures failed to work because there had been a structural shift in industrial activity. No longer was the effort to increase output and capacity receiving the bulk of investment dollars. Instead, those dollars were now plowed back into automation and new technology in order to replace workers and thus reduce costs. This shift of emphasis became one big reason for the high unemployment rate in 1980-1984. By the early 1980s about 65% of total capital investment was going for greater technological efficiency (labor displacement), and only 35% for augmenting the capacity upon which living standards depend.[2]

Constant talk about capital shortages by business executives, Chase Bank, Citibank and editorials in the *Wall Street Journal* and other financial news outlets ignored this structural change. They clung instead to the now obsolete supply-side economic concept—that business investment generates demand for both consumer and capital goods, through wages for workers in the former and demand for machines in the latter. It seemed an ideal and self-generating process. The produced goods would be purchased by consumers and newly employed workers, stimulating new demand, and so on into a happy spiral. The trouble was, the theory didn't fit the reality—factories can order tools without increasing their work force.

So the main reason Keynesian theory fit less well in he 1980s was due to the net effect capital was having on employment. For twenty years investment in technology merely lowered employment in those factories buying labor-saving machines. Now, in the age of robotics, investment can replace the worker altogether, killing Keynesian theory.

There has also been a little-noticed shift in U.S. manufacturing sectors like clothing and steel to high technology and low productivity. Most economists did not realize this was going on. While the power economists wrongly insisted on tax cuts and more spending, the shift predictably interrupted industrial growth and old patterns of production. Proof? Manufacturing product, which grew at about a 6.5% rate in the early 1960s, fell to 4.7% in 1970-73. From 1973-76 it fell to 0%. Yes, zero. In steel, textiles and light manufacturing (like TVs) it was a minus in 1977. And we saw our traditional labor intensive manufacturing move to less developed countries like Taiwan, Korea and Mexico.

Psychology Takes Over

This is major trend number three. Increasingly, in financial circles and in the media, we heard and read of psychological influences. We read in the press that this or that event was caused by "rising confidence," "loss of public or private confidence," etc. There actually has been a lot of research on the psychological causes of business cycles. However, psychology is rarely the main cause. Rather, it is an important secondary cause which aggravates economic trends begun by internal technical forces.

"Waves of elation and discouragement sweep over the business community. This comes about through two principal influences. First, apart from financial ties by which businessmen are bound together, there exists among them a certain measure of psychological interdependence. A change of tone in one part of the business world diffuses itself, in a quite unreasoning manner, over other and wholly disconnected parts. Second, an error of optimism on the part of one group of businessmen itself creates a justification for some improved expectations on the part of other groups. [For example, the president of General Motors publicly predicted that 1978 would be a "socko year" for auto sales, even in the face of a 10% decline]. The optimistic error once born grows in scope and magnitude."[3]

Economist A. C. Pigou continued,

"But, since the prosperity has been built primarily upon error, a day of reckoning must come. This day does not dawn until after a time long enough to construct new industrial equipment on a large scale, to bring the products of the new equipment to market, and to find that they cannot be disposed of promptly at profitable prices [like 1987 Chevrolets at $12,000]. The past miscalculations become patent—patent to creditors as well as to debtors, and in dying it gives birth to an error of pessimism. This new error is born not an infant but a giant. An industrial boom has necessarily been a period of strong emotional excitement, and an excited man passes from one form of excitement to another more rapidly than he passes to quiesence. Under the influence of the new error, business is unduly depressed."[4]

Prices and Profits Cannot Support the Debt Load

Major trend number four: crushing debt.

The central problem was the total debt unpaid. Few of the brand name economists address crushing debt.

During the furious debt inflation in the U.S. and the world from 1975 to 1981, corporations, consumers, and governments were able to use rising prices (and rising wages and taxes) to assist in servicing a steadily rising debt load. Rising prices insure rising cash flows in all sectors, and have made debt problems appear easy. For instance, a vice president[5] of Ford Motor Company wrote me in 1977 saying that the key to their success was price inflation (not styling). Well, of course, this insured profits by netting more per unit. When production slipped, their profits still held up. So long as prices continued to rise, the debt problem could be put on the back burner until debt service grew to equal profit.

FALLING PRICES

But when prices fell, the squeeze became greater at all levels in managing debt, because, remember, it has been ever rising prices that supported the enormous debt in the first place. A point is reached, however, where additional credits will accumulate and not be used because neither lender nor borrower has any confidence in taking further risks.

In addition, the corporate economic gimmick of administering prices and having them sticky on the high side, finally failed. In 1978 the steel industry raised prices at a time when 23,000 workers were idle, plants were operating at 74% capacity and Japanese steel was swamping them. Large corporations defied an old economic law which says that when demand falls, you lower prices to restore demand.

FALLING PROFITS

Corporate bottomline profits have been on a downtrend for twenty years or so, even while a major source of profits has been interest collected on debts. When the debts are not repaid, and defaults become large, profits disappear. In addition, profits per se are not important in a high debt context. The significant figure becomes total cash flow. The size of the debt problem was staggering: by 1986 Sears, for example, had their credit cards in the hands of roughly one out of every three Americans. With 70% of their sales on credit, they were extraordinarily vulnerable.

REFLATION PANACEA

The first thing policymakers do when deflation (sagging prices) becomes apparent is to devise new ways to reflate (deliberately reverse the price slide). Some policymakers, seeing this need in the early 1980s, proposed reflation as follows:

1. Install a new world currency to be called BANCOR, SDR or ECU. It would be more fiat paper money, but this time on a world scale. Supposedly it would solve the debt service and repayment problem like magic. Paper money has not succeeded in this task since the beginning of time, but hope springs eternal, so the idea was seriously considered.

2. Demonetize gold (get gold out of people's hands as a store of value). There is much evidence that this could not (and will not) work, since gold remains one of the few places to store money.

3. Allow the dollar to fall sharply as a store of value. Substitute the Bank of International Settlements (BIS) for the International Monetary Fund (IMF) as a world bank of last resort. This idea of such a world Federal Reserve Bank was thinking big, indeed.

It was assumed that somehow the crushing world debt loads could be paid off with this new fiat money, or abundant domestic paper currencies (U.S. dollars). Either or both would reflate prices and put us back on a rising price curve again. But the numbers were enormous and deflation's slide to the crash was too strong—akin to the "irresistible force and immovable object." So reflation on a scale to do the job would have been astronomical. Like special drawing rights, another world currency idea that came along a few years ago, reflation was doomed.

Can reflation work if demand sours? No. It was a failure when attempted during the Great Depression. Some say it didn't succeed then because the effort wasn't big enough. But the fact is, it didn't succeed because no one wanted to risk borrowing or lending or launching new ventures. Everyone was depressed mentally.

Now we are beginning to see a similar psychological mood, a lack of confidence about what tomorrow will bring. No demand in the 1930s meant no money in use. We came then, and have come again, to the idle money syndrome. The banks had plenty but nobody wanted to borrow it. Interest rates fell to almost zero, and debt liquidation proceeded at full scale. Both currency and credit money are promises. Both are lent at a rate of interest. Could reflation—even with bales of world paper money—have succeeded between 1979 and 1985? No. The plan was doomed before it was born.

To turn the economy around from the serious recession of 1973–75, the Fed, with major private banks lending, chose reflation. The U.S. dollar fell dramatically as credit was created at rates unparalleled in U.S. economic history—or the history of the world, for that matter. Heavy credit expansion during the Nixon recession of 1970 was small compared with the artificial steps taken in the late 1970s to create more "credit" and therefore debt.

The *Wall Street Journal* in December 1977 stated, "Total private borrowing has risen 185% since March, 1973, the low of the recession. That compares with an average rise of 71% for the same interval in four previous recessions. Arthur Burns estimated total credit was running, in the third quarter of 1977, at an annual rate of $400 billion, about $90 billion more than a year earlier."[6]

The reason is found in the laws of physics: the mass was bigger, taking more to move it. But then, with prices and total demand declining, with the dollar artificially strong to attract foreign money to support the U.S. federal debt and trade deficits, there was no way this private-sector debt dinosaur could be repaid. A severe liquidity squeeze is inevitable when demand and hope prod each other downward. Cash flow would decline and debt could no longer be repaid. When this crisis reaches its peak, call money quickly shoots to 20%, just as it did in the 1920s, signaling to all that "this is it!"

Major Trend Number Five:
The We-Conquered-Hard-Times Delusion

Americans under forty years of age have no personal experience with the hard time economics of 1929 to 1942. Those over forty, especially economic policymakers who were raised during those hard times, hoped to erase this prospect from their minds. Therefore, after forty years of rising curves, we all came to believe that we were the first society to conquer the centuries-long scourge of hard times: depressed economic conditions. We also thought that America was unique—our spectacular technology was always ahead, ready to save the day, and our economic curve was always rising.

Jean Gimpel, a scholar of medieval history, shatters the above notion in his book *The Medieval Machine*. The major reason we believed that "we are the first" was found in the character of our high school history lessons. (Events and people were traditional and superficial. Deeper currents were selectively taught. Few historians have studied the history of technology, Gimpel says, because they preferred to show man as a worker—working with his hands, making the world move, and such.)

The ten-year-old energy crisis precipitated most of the public concern for economic and financial matters. It even awakened, again, the fear of depression and made many people apprehensive that Western technological society could be doomed to decline and perish like all the world's previous civilizations. Gimpel asks, "Will our machine technics, our railways, cars, ships and airplanes disappear before the Roman roads and the Wall of China? Even our skyscrapers in ruins as in Babylon?"[7]

As Oswald Spengler wrote years ago, "The history of this technics is fast drawing to an inevitable close. It will be eaten from within like the grand forms of any and every culture."[8]

The Middle Ages, Gimpel discovered, was one of the great inventive eras of mankind. Between the tenth and thirteenth centuries, Western Europe experienced a technological boom. Both that boom and subsequent decline offer striking parallels to Western industrial society since 1750, the pre-crash situation in the United States. Some features of this first industrial revolution seem strangely familiar:

1. Great increase in population; new lands were colonized, new towns built.

2. Conditions favored free enterprise, leading to the rise of the self-made man.

3. Capitalist companies were formed and their shares sold.

4. Ruthless business methods were introduced to stifle competition.

5. There was an extensive division of labor and strikes by workers.

6. Energy consumption increased strikingly.

7. The use of machines was greatly expanded; tasks formerly done by hand were done by machines.

8. Simultaneously there was a revolution in agriculture.

9. The general standard of living rose.

10. The growth of industry led to extensive pollution, posing a threat to the environment with long-term consequences.

11. Entrepreneurs extracted large profits, and developed accounting and banking techniques.

12. The period was characterized by a spirit of optimism, a rationalist attitude and a firm belief in progress.

Sound familiar? But at a certain point, the dynamism of the Middle Ages began to fail, and symptoms of decline became evident. The population ceased to grow, differences between the classes hardened, there was less social mobility. Restrictive practices were introduced in many industries. Unrest grew in large industrial centers. The level of efficiency was dropping while at the same time there was great resistance to change. Energy production had peaked, and the standard of living began to decline. Inflation began to get out of hand, currencies were devalued and banks crashed. Established moral values declined. People became less public spirited and more permissive. Many turned from traditional religion to embrace new esoteric cults.

In recent pre-crash years there has been much written around Professor Gimpel's theme: the industrial society we take for granted may end, and we will spend the balance of our lives in a service society, where some familiar values will automatically become obsolete. There was certainly plenty of evidence that this corner was being turned, as I and others have written.[9] But I do not intend to infer that the new age we have turned a corner into will be as bad as it may first appear. It will, however, be different.

Here, in summary, are the major trends that have moved our economy from 1978 to 1987–88:

1. The long term decline in liquidity

2. The death of demand management

3. Psychology takes over

4. Prices and profits unable to support the debt load

5. The delusion that we conquered hard times

Seen from the Long Term, It's Disaster Ahead

To make sense out of the half century between 1945 and 2000, we must think about major fundamental changes that have taken place in our economic structure and process. It is important (1) to not be swayed by short-run economic news or data (which is most often revised heavily); (2) to ignore almost all mass media business and economic analysis; these entertainers do not know and therefore cannot tell you what is significant (the truth); and (3) to know what long-term trends prevail.

This three-century inventive era is unfamiliar because the history of technology has been neglected, thanks largely to the hoary attitudes of academics and intellectuals regarding manual work and engineering. These same ivory tower priests have failed to solve our current economic crisis. But that comes as no surprise, since such conformist scholars also failed to solve past crises.

TECHNOLOGICAL ATROPHY

The Russian economist Kondratieff noticed this phenomenon earlier in this century. He found, by examining historically detailed data, that any industrial nation's technological foundation changes in a predictable pattern, or cycle. As cycles go, these are long, lasting about fifty to sixty-five years. When they peak, after exhausting the potential of the technical base, the succeeding technology is too immature to attract and absorb giant investments. The nation's economy will coast, then slide into a depression phase.

We are now beginning a depression phase. We are between technological bases which attract enough capital to produce nation-sized goods and services. We have been coasting on a mature technological base for fifteen-plus years. From the edge of that plateau, we have just dropped into the valley, where we really can't see clearly the next plateau. Of all relevant traditional cycles, this Kondratieff Wave most resembles a historical economic pendulum.

The Middle Ages ended with an economic depression in the fourteenth century. That slump lasted for a hundred years and was followed ultimately by technological and economic recovery. "But" says Gimpel, "the depression we have moved into will have no end. There will be no further industrial revolution in the cycles of our Western Civilization."[10]

GREED: IT'S AGES OLD

American history is replete with manias and panics: land manias, railroad booms and busts, stock market manias and so on. These are generally associated with the psychology of mobs. All at once, out of the blue, men go berserk, driven by fear, and behave crazily. Gustav Le Bon discussed this phenomenon in his book, *The Crowd*. This phenomenon is driven by the two over-riding emotions: greed and fear.

Americans, collectively, caught the greed fever some time during the 1970s. The inflation that then erupted made men more greedy. Americans came to revere greed. This was depicted in a TV series, "The Lifestyles of the Rich and Famous," an obscene portrayal of a human failure, greed. Economic and social history is awash with this curious behavior.

Inevitably some unforeseen event transforms greed into fear, in a flash. Suddenly men become irrational, and in a last-ditch effort to save their financial skins, they sell what they own and rush for cash.

The coming panic, it seems to me, will be unique in both its size and fallout. Never before in U.S. history have our bankers loaned out so much of our resources to foreigners who will never repay. In the late 1920s individual Americans bought Mexican bonds, $1 billion worth. When Mexico defaulted (no Latin nation has repaid a debt since 1800) those citizens lost what they'd loaned. This time around, it is far different. The average American with deposits in a hometown bank does not know that his money was loaned to foreigners who will never repay.

When this is discovered by the public, it will cause fears to blaze. And the American rich will discover they have shot themselves in their own feet by allowing money-center bankers to lend their funds, never to be repaid. It's not difficult to foresee the episodic changes this will bring in its wake. We abused the use of credit. It will, in turn, abuse us.

As it says in Ecclesiastes 8-10: "Like fish

caught up in a net, like a bird taken in a snare, *so men are trapped when bad times come suddenly."*

BANK CREDIT AND THE PRIVATE SECTOR

The common thread running through past financial panics was the overextension of bank credit. Everyone seems to have forgotten the dependency factor, the fact that everyone depends on someone else to provide income. When whoever you depend on for income cannot provide it, you are unable to fulfill your financial obligations.

Most of the credit card debt, honestly acquired, is a time bomb. It's highly unstable and ready to explode with defaults en masse. Over $600 billion was owed by late 1987 on the installment plan by American consumers. Nothing changes. This particular situation has surfaced again and again in American history. The one constant is human behavior. Thus we repeat our mistakes, generation after generation.

The system will not change as long as we don't. For this basic, simple reason, the money acquired while the economic curve was rising will be lost when the curve falls and the bad debts become unpayable by either borrower or lender.

The best time to be rich is not in good times, but in hard times. In America the only thing we pile up in large numbers in good times is debt. In bad times those with the cash plant the seeds of future fortunes.

CHAPTER 4

ECONOMICS IGNORES YOU

Capitalism's Human Flaw

The fact that depressions continue to occur despite preventive efforts, despite the U.S. government and Federal Reserve, tells us, among other things, that our ability to control the economy is no better today than it was in 1929. One might therefore reasonably ask if there is some fatal flaw in capitalism—either its creation or execution.

In a real sense, the concept of capitalism is flawed because it is operated for and by human beings. Some will ignore the operating essentials of capitalism and become hypnotized by the element which facilitates capitalism and is also its alluring by-product: money.

American society has transformed this alluring by-product into personal power. We have forgotten that money's chief function is to make the machine go. Why do we honor money claims? Because our whole society is profoundly convinced that money is good in and of itself; that it is good for society no less than for individuals;

indeed, that social progress itself depends upon the accumulation of money.

The latter is a necessary, but not sufficient, essential of capitalism. Unfortunately for all of us, it leads us astray. In reality, social progress depends upon the ability to enlarge the productive apparatus. But since, in a commercial society, money will buy anything, those who control accumulations of money are in a position to buy and control the increasing of productive apparatus that spells social progress. Therefore it appears to most that money is the instrument of progress.

Capital has two definitions. Capital is the money that capitalists accumulate, and it is also the physical plant of industry that engineers design and workmen build with materials that other workmen fabricate with previously designed and built industrial plants. Both accumulations of money and industrial plants are capital—and blessed they are, for without them no economic progress is possible.

Progress, as an idea, is potent. Our society has been dominated by progress and human perfectibility for something like four centuries. Little wonder that the mechanism came to be known more than personal power. It is productive power. By accumulating money we gather power for either purpose. And our motives for its accumulation are independent of society.

OVER-ACCUMULATION

It would be miraculous if that motive didn't lead to over-accumulation. And, of course, we know that it does. Evidence has been compiled to show that the rate of money accumulation was accelerating throughout the supposed prosperity of the 1920s, reaching a climax in 1929, when three times as much money was accumulated in the U.S. as could be absorbed by real industrial expansion.

This money bought nothing. This money, estimated to be $6 billion in 1929, was laid out for inflated security values by a process of pseudo-investment. Instead of buying goods and services, that $6 billion overfilled a credit balloon—which then burst, plunging the country into the Great Depression.

Though we recognize that capitalism must accumulate funds for production, rarely do we worry about over-accumulation. Instead, we are told, as in 1983, that there is a shortage of investment opportunities. Thus, Reaganomics cut taxes so the proceeds would somehow wind up in new investments.

Where is the evidence that we had another over-accumulation of capital in the early 1980s? Guy E. Noyes, a former senior vice president and economist for Morgan Guaranty Trust Company, noted that by the end of 1980 the annual rate of withdrawals from accounts (e.g., your own bank deposit balance) at banks was about $68 trillion. But the GNP was running at $2.7 trillion a year. Thus, only 4% of the work being done by money was related to transactions in goods and services that make up GNP. As Noyes explained:

"A large volume of transactions, not counted in the 4% figure, involves intermediate purchases of goods and services as opposed to final purchases, which is what GNP measures. However, financial payments represented far and away the great bulk of total debits to demand deposits."[1]

The implication here is that before the impending crash most of the money in the economy circulated in the financial sector. Those who talk about lack of savings as the cause of our present economic troubles should ponder this fact. This hyper-extension of the financial sector results in swelling the financial bubble to the breaking point, which always leads to a chain-reaction financial collapse and panic. Over-accumulation of capital was seen in the over $200 billion size of the money market funds, and the massive $9 trillion in debt in the private sector.

Since capitalism seems to encourage finances to run ahead of production, credit accumulates excessively—creating a credit bubble which always bursts. This credit instability was shown in rapid frenzy increased financial markets, stocks and commodities. Equity mortgages unlocked $1.9 trillion frozen in housing capital, becoming additional funds for the speculative binge. Very similar to 1929.

Finally, it is a common belief that economic growth turns primarily on the accumulation of capital through the savings and investment process. Edward Dennison of the Brookings Institution has spent a lifetime studying the causes of economic growth. In his book *Accounting for U.S. Economic Growth 1929–1969*, he concluded that labor accounted for 17% of total growth, capital for just 24% and advances in knowledge for an astounding 34%.

So, again, established economists walk up a dark alley with supply-side theory dedicated to capital formation (and/or accumulation). To make matters worse, the Reagan budget for 1983 proposed a 50% cut in student aid. That move in our information-based, high technology society practically guarantees that the coming depression will be prolonged, by curtailing the growth-of-knowledge machine which drives our economy.

THE ACCUMULATION PROCESS

The distribution of wealth in our form of economic system has always been uneven. This is true in all societies, in all times, as I noted earlier. But since 1945, the distribution of income appears to be growing even more uneven. A study made by the Joint Economic Committee of Congress in 1983 shows this, as you can see from this chart:

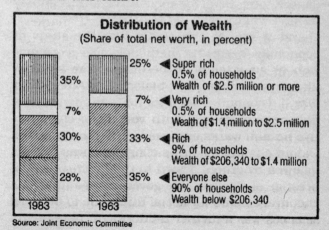

Distribution of Wealth
(Share of total net worth, in percent)

1983	1963	
35%	25%	◀ Super rich 0.5% of households Wealth of $2.5 million or more
7%	7%	◀ Very rich 0.5% of households Wealth of $1.4 million to $2.5 million
30%	33%	◀ Rich 9% of households Wealth of $206,340 to $1.4 million
28%	35%	◀ Everyone else 90% of households Wealth below $206,340

Source: Joint Economic Committee

The public does not object. As a matter of fact, like it or not, Joseph Pechman of the Brookings Institution wrote in his book *Federal Tax Policy*, "A surprising number [of the public] resent even the relatively low taxes imposed on estates as large as $1 million, because many people consider weaith to be the family home, their car, personal savings, and similar property not regarded as appropriate objects of taxation."

So we must take things as they are for now, at least - even though a listing of the four hundred richest people in America may gall you.

Established Economics

It is taught in the universities, proliferated in journals and regurgituted in councils of government, yet established economics, with all its mountains of published outputs, has not advanced our capacity to control our economy beyond what it was in the 1930s.

And it was in the 1930s that the study of economics began its methodological reorientation in an attempt to become a true science, like physics, chemistry, biology, etc. After World War II, economics shed its tie to human values and became neutral with respect to comparative human wants and needs. Sir John Hicks of Oxford championed this effort, and was eagerly followed by others drawn to the exactitude and prestige of science. The government's financial encouragements for social discipline to become sciences was a further inducement, not only to economics but to sociology, psychology and cultural anthropology.

Obviously, this successful effort to dehumanize the discipline largely explains why economics ignores us mere mortals today. As if that wasn't enough, this new, value-free study was carried into mathematical expression by way of Paul Samuelson's book *Foundation of Economic Analysis.* He intended to recast economic theory into mathematical propositions which could be verified or refuted through experimental tests. It's interesting to note that to date none of these propositions has been so tested. What we have, then, is surely not a science. Its fundamental methodology is incomplete because the acceptance or rejection of this dehumanized, complex, esoteric, mathematical symbolism still relies on intuitive judgment. And intuitive judgment requires less hard-data cerebral activity than deciding when to cross a busy street.

REAGAN VS. ESTABLISHED ECONOMISTS

Not everyone was happy with Reaganomics, including those who knew that the shift in tax burden from corporations to private citizens was continuing and even accelerating during this administration. Those who applauded the campaign slogan, "Get government off our backs," did not suspect it would decrease life-giving benefits to less fortunate citizens both young and old. Odd, this administration ignored human needs at the same time it ignored economists who also ignored human needs.

Twenty-twenty hindsight shows balanced budgets far superior to backbreaking deficits.

Established economists failed to show President Reagan anything he felt he needed to conceive and carry out the most economically creative administration in recent memory. And it does appear that Mr. Reagan has kept those sterile mathematicians at arms length—prior to the inevitable crash. Several excerpts from a *New York Times* article "Behind Reagan's Economic Shuffle," suffice to illuminate the failure of establishment economists to make themselves useful:

"The mainstream economic nay-sayers, who warned that the record budget deficits would explode in Mr. Reagan's face, are still waiting for that to happen. In fact, as a group economists have failed to predict most of the important economic trends of recent years. Inaccurate forecasts should not come as a surprise.

"By and large, economists failed to anticipate the rapid and sustained drop in inflation. They did not expect the recovery to survive high interest rates and a huge deficit. And they were wildly wrong in predicting, time and again over the past year or so, the imminent collapse of the dollar from what they thought were unsustainable highs. 'It's no wonder,' said John Makin, director of fiscal policy studies at the American Enterprise Institute, 'that the President's attitude toward economists has gone from negative to more negative.'

"Economists in general persisted in viewing the United States as a self-contained whole, long after businessmen, for example, had recognized that the country was increasingly tied to the global economy. They did not adequately consider, for example, the fact that high interest rates and an improved climate for business in the United States would attract such huge amounts of foreign capital.

"Modern economists have been hurt by their tendency to focus evermore on refining mathematical technique rather than on rethinking their key analytic assumptions."

The article concludes with a quote from one Mr. Albertine, who said, "I think it's abundantly clear that as influence-peddlers economists are now very close to zero."[2]

Zero, indeed. Mr. Reagan, when once asked whether he considered himself an economist, leaned back in his wingback chair and guffawed, "I've been called bad names before, but never economist."

"BUT ECONOMISTS . . . ?

How sad that such a potentially useful calling should be brought to the low estate of a "bad name." Is there a better light in which to view this mortally wounded discipline? Must it be rebuilt virtually from scratch, erasing the dehumanization of John Hicks and the mathematical purity of Samuelson? Knowing modern mankind's repudiation of history and fascination with machines, is it realistic to believe that classical, historical economics could become the foundation for rational planning?

There are shining examples of state and local governments that do so. They even use the power of computers to store, assemble, manipulate and present data; to compare, measure and select from options; to identify dominant paths and secure several likelihoods; to extrapolate and project; to monitor and provide mid-course guidance—but in a gross, sterile abstraction whose roots are experimental formulas, not in a grand model related to human life as it is lived.

WHAT WILL THEY SAY AFTER THE CRASH?

So here we are after the crash, the shocked, even terrified victims of the clear failure of neoclassical and Keynesian concepts, and of techniques for monetary and fiscal control . . . a nation left with no clear answer for how and why we got here and what we are to do now.

And the establishment economists, in their silence or confusion—what are they to say? Let's speculate:

1. "We were caught by surprise too."

2. "We knew, but didn't want to frighten anyone."

3. "We knew, but the President wouldn't listen."

4. "We knew, but wanted to make a bundle in the collapse."

5. "We suspected the economy was very sick but didn't want to rock the official boat."

6. "We establishment economists didn't cause it, so why beat on us?"

7. "We didn't have the President's ear, so the Federal Reserve is to blame."

8. "Don't worry, we'll all be the better for a little temporary discomfort—cleans us out, purifies."

Well, we could go on and on with such finger pointing after the crash, and no doubt will. But how will we get out of the mess? If the concepts and tools of the establishment economists were too flawed to catch a really big fifty- to sixty-year event, how can they possibly help put the world back together afterward? A crisis of confidence. Or, if they knew but didn't tell us, how can they be trusted to help build a new economic world in which a sensible person can be useful and creative? A crisis of trust. Or, if the collapse was all part of establishment economic planning, just as the rebuilding must be . . . a crisis of value.

There will be no point in asking brand name economists to help create a future that affirms life, where trust and values among humans speak of sharing and not fearful isolation. Sir John Hicks stripped economics of human needs and wants, and Paul Samuelson recast economic theory in mathematical propositions.

The late Joan Robinson, a Cambridge University economist not recognized by the Nobel Award givers, has the following to say about the mathematical models upon which G.M., the Fed, Ford, the White House, and all major banks lean as they blindly stagger into the future:

"Mathematical operations are performed upon entities that cannot be defined; calculations are made in terms of units that cannot be measured; accounting identities are mistaken for functional relationships; correlations are mistaken for causal laws; differences are identified with changes; and one-way movements in time are treated like movements to and fro in space. The complexity of models is elaborated merely for display, far and away beyond the possible application to reality."[3]

No, we cannot return any semblance of control to establishment economists and their mathematical models "far and away beyond the application to reality." I believe we will feel like fools, or worse—madhouse prisoners—

when, after the crash, we realize they did not help us foresee mild fluctuations in business, let alone big cyclical collapses. We will be angry.

CHAPTER 5

THE RISE
OF A
BANK CREDIT SOCIETY

All of us, I'm sorry to say—man on the street and economist alike—have taken credit for granted at worst, and been confused by it at best. Isn't credit money? No. But we use it as money, either ignoring the difference or being ignorant of it.

What is the difference?

Money is an asset you own. Credit is an asset you owe. And upon which you pay interest. You borrowed it, usually from a bank, which thereupon created it out of thin air. (The bank had no gold or silver bars to lend you, or even to hold in your name.)

Much ignorance and confusion about credit has grown since 1945, and especially since 1970, when credit card use expanded dramatically. Not having been taught to make a distinction, we have thought of money as coins, currency and bank deposits (checkbook money). But how much of that is really currency and coin? Only 5%. The other 95% is bank-credit money, including your deposit balance from paychecks at the bank, balances that came into being when you made a loan from the bank and it was credited to your account, and your savings account balance.

There are other credit substitutes for money, such as certificates of deposit, commercial paper, etc., and these amount to vast sums.

Finally, there is the paper money we speak of as printed by the Bureau of Printing and Engraving (on Treasury orders); Federal Reserve notes.

Indeed, the Fed does pay the U.S. Treasury to print and coin money, which the Fed then circulates and on which we also pay interest, since Federal Reserve notes must have as collateral U.S. Treasury bonds, which are interest-paying IOUs.

Credit Cards and Personal Checks

As consumers we are billed for goods and services, from tires to telephones. Some of these bills are paid with checks, and others with credit cards. In our collective mind the difference has become increasingly fuzzy, although in reality it's 18 to 20%.

What began as a right to use a credit card has become, in essence, a credit check on an individual. Our line of credit at the bank (the credit card limit) is supposed to be proof that we are good for the amount we charge. When we use a personal check to make a purchase, the seller often demands to see our credit card, and may accept it as both identification and as an assurance that our check is backed by good credit.

Thus, one debt is supporting another, even guaranteeing the good credit of another. This is also the case with our paper money, the Federal Reserve notes and coins which are guaranteed by those IOUs called U.S. Treasury bonds.

Now this iron fairyweb which debt has woven in our society lurks below our level of consciousness and looks harmless enough on the surface. But it has us all caught. It all looks harmless enough on the surface, but there is always lurking in the background—almost hidden—this iron weave of debt, waiting for the diamond-sharp laws of economics to take effect.

CREDIT'S HISTORY

Though always inherently unstable, bank credit is not new in economic history. With it feudal kings made war and great mercantile houses traded goods and built colonies throughout the known world. What is new in our time is the extraordinary development of bank credit in the private sector. No longer is it confined to kings and merchant princes—now it's for ordinary consumers.

Having acquired the right to use credit, we consumers will use all we are allotted and then some. We consumers do not like to think of repayment, nor of high interest rates. Our God-given right to consume made the distribution of credit cards a sure-fire profit maker from the beginning.

Consumer credit seems infinitely expandable. Once these avenues of credit expansion are opened, controls and restraints disappear, and sooner or later the economy is supported by credit alone.

That expansion is, however, not infinite. It will be stopped by a fore-ordained long-term credit contraction, an event that began long ago. And which climaxed after the OPEC rout in October 1984. Again, like the cartoon character Pogo stated, "We has met the enemy and it is us."

In 1980 President Carter became alarmed by the rapid rise in consumer credit via credit cards. The controls he imposed cut credit use, and thus business income at the retail level. It was a sharp and bona fide event, and it brought on a mini-recession.

It's interesting to note that since 1980 no policymaker has dared restrict any form of credit. And as we moved toward the inevitable crash, consumers ignored a traditional market force—high interest rates. They became meaningless, lost their power; everyone seemed to take them for granted. Did we really believe the credit bubble was infinitely expandable?

Instability:
"The Fed Controls Money Supply"

Both popular wisdom and economic theory today has the Federal Reserve controlling the money supply. Here's how the American Banking Association described the process:

> "The Federal Reserve Act requires that member banks keep a certain reserve against their deposits. The reserve is figured as a percentage of deposits, for example, 20%. Reserves are kept in cash in the bank's vault, and on deposit with the nearest Federal Reserve Bank. Thus a bank cannot increase its deposits without adding to its reserve. And, since loans create deposits, it cannot make loans without increasing reserves (unless it has some unused reserves)."

Simply put, deposits depend on reserves, loans create deposits, loans depend on reserves. To continue with the American Banking Association description:

> "Reserves are the key to bank credit, and the Federal Reserve holds the reserves. The Federal Reserve can create the reserves and pump them into the banking system. This action enables banks to make loans, if they wish. Or, the Federal Reserve can withdraw reserves from the banking system,

which may cause banks to cut down on their loans."[1]

That's current theory. It is the gospel that economists from everywhere in the academic spectrum preached in the halcyon days of the 1970s and 1980s. As an example, Citibank wrote "If and when the FED relaxes, the effect would be to push down the FED funds rate, which has been abnormally high."[2] By "relaxes," what is meant is that the Fed purchases enough government IOUs to become a major addition to the banking system's reserves, which can then be used to back more loans.

ORDINARY THEORY

The founders of the Federal Reserve in 1913 had an identical view of the use of reserves to control bank lending. In the beginning it was believed that if the reserve requirement was 25% and it was suddenly raised to 35%, bank lending would immediately shrink. Conversely, if the reserve were lowered by 10%, banks could make more credit available.

Besides declaring changes in reserve requirements, the Fed is empowered to tighten reserves by "draining the system," by selling government bonds on the open market. It was, and is, believed that fewer reserves in the banking system will cause banks to lend less, and conversely, the expansion of reserves causes banks to lend more.

From 1913 to 1980 the required reserve levels dropped steadily, and under the Monetary Act of 1980 were lowered to 12%. By 1984 they were allowed to fall still more to ensure the steady creation and expansion of credit.

But even more significant are the many types of credit which have no reserve requirement, and are quickly available to banks. The most glaring example is the Eurodollar market, a vast $2 trillion credit pool readily accessible by money center banks, no *reserve required!*

Despite the Fed's original theory and practice, it has for most of its history encouraged credit creation. And it has encouraged the passage of laws to expand credit. It could be argued that the Fed had lost control over the credit bubble even before 1977 while it was still largely a U.S. system. After the system became international, the Fed could only talk control. Its historic instruments designed for that purpose no longer worked.

Now the multi-trillion-dollar world credit bubble is a monster of fantasy proportions. It's much larger than its supporting financial structure's ability to earn down its principle, let alone pay the bloated, still swelling interest burden it carries. While the credit monster and its sack of interest was still within human comprehension, the Fed could have been likened to a powerful tiger. Today the tiger is a pussy cat.

Was the Fed doomed from the beginning in its appointed task of controlling the freedom-loving banks? Economic growth did require credit. And financial houses, like children, want their own way; they want to grow, test, reach for their limit. Like children, they will seek special advantage, devise self-serving tricks and scamper for protection when in trouble.

Once U.S. money center banks learned to meet the Fed's parental rules in token gestures and escaped to play in the green pastures of the real-time, worldwide money shuffle, even the pretense of control was over. The Fed as parent can no longer save its children from the credit monster they helped create.

POPULISTS VS. HARD MONEY

The history of both economic theory and actual practice always has reflected a clash between the so-called Currency School (also labeled Hard Money, Monetarism, and lately the Chicago School) and the Banking School (championed by Populists and Keynesians).

Professor Charles Kindelberger of MIT, in his book *Manias, Panics and Crashes* described this on-going battle:

"In the 1800s in the United States, more or less the same breakdown in ideology and economic analysis separated the hard money school from the Populists. In the eyes of most economists, the Currency School of 1810 won a clear intellectual victory over its opposition . . .

"The clash between forces seeking to limit the money supply (the Currency School) and those wanting or at least acting to expand it (the Banking School) goes back at least a hundred years. Some institutions rendered a given money supply more efficient. Others expanded it.

"If the Banking School was right on the need for credit expansion to make a start in economic expansion, the Currency School was surely correct in observing that credit creation based thereafter on ongoing business opportunities is a formula for disaster."[3]

From the Great Depression to 1960, Keynesian theories held sway in academic and administrative circles. Since then, Monetarists of the Chicago School have dominated ivory-tower thinking. Then their star vanished from the galaxy of economic ideas, and supply-side economic ideas moved in—and out.

THEORY VS. REAL WORLD

Despite glorious cerebrations in the Chicago School, the real world seems to have eagerly followed the Banking School in the creation of credit money—and far beyond the need to make a start in economic expansion. Both schools and the real world know that credit money is fluid and difficult to control. Or was go-go banking blind to this truism in 1960 when Walter Wriston, former chairman of Citibank, invented the now-famous certificate of deposit, which allowed banks to create their own credit?

Banks were allowed to form their own holding companies. These were new companies which then owned the underlying bank and which could engage in many financial activities. This then brought yet another new development; permitting banks to sell their own commercial paper (corporate IOUs given for credit). Finally the Eurodollar and its credits became available to everyone. Thus did private banks provide themselves with an overwhelming credit-creating force to diminish or destroy forever the Federal Reserve's power to control its member banks' fatal fascination with growth.

And growth they achieved. Deposit liabilities of commercial banks were reported at $4.1 billion in 1900. By 1910 the figure was $14.6 billion. In 1970 it was $436.6 billion, and by March of 1986 it was $1.75 trillion, according to the *Federal Reserve Bulletin* of that year. This is an increase of over 320 times in 84 years. So much for the application of hard money theories from the Chicago School's ivory tower.

Consumer Psychology

The post-war domestic credit bubble is the creature of a three-way symbiosis:

1. Banking's fixation on growth

2. Madison Avenue and politicians' helping the public pursue happiness

3. The response of Mr. Average Wage Earner, who came to feel he deserved to possess what he could pay for only by borrowing against his future income

Advertisers and politicians can't extend credit, obviously, but they are great catalysts. In the final analysis, this last great U.S. credit expansion depended on consumer psychology. The mood of the public, its willingness to borrow, was teased by good-time ads and coaxed by ready credit. Oblivious to the long-term consequences, the public succumbed to these blandishments and consumed (or squandered) 65% of the GNP from 1945 through 1984—mostly by credit purchases.

CHAPTER 6

THE CREATION
OF
FICTIONAL MONEY

Capitalism is now suffering its second paralytic stroke, following a series of minor strokes in the nineteenth and twentieth centuries. All featured collapsing credit. However, the crash of 1929 and this one are different enough in degree to be different in kind. Restoring world capitalism to health, if possible, will require remedies also different in kind.

As Dr. Nicholas Murray Butler, a lifelong friend and counselor of capitalism, said:

"The economic, the social and the political convolutions which are shaking the whole world are without parallel in history. It is quite futile to draw curves and to make charts of how earlier depressions and economic crises in the United States have developed and how they have led the way to recovery. This procedure is wholly futile because conditions are entirely without precedent and the remedies for these conditions will have to be without precedent as well."[1]

While very ill, American capitalism is not going to die. But, like most stroke victims, it will never be quite the same as it was before. Some would argue that American capitalism is so flawed that it should be laid to rest and replaced with a different and better economic model. Most of us can appreciate the seeming merit of that argument. However, in agreeing with it, we forget we have only old, failed and localized experience with other traditions. No, restoration will be in a capitalistic framework—we have nothing to take its place.

Not only do we have no national experience with other economic models, we have groups espousing advanced social thought in England, France and Germany. It is hard to imagine a basic change in our social structure. Certainly neither can be accomplished in our immediate future without the strong support of public opinion. And remember that the public in crisis tends to conservatism, not radicalism; to affirmation of traditional attitudes and values rather than their abandonment. As a nation, we will not become the Donner party. So we may just as well start to help capitalism pull itself together.

A History of Faith in Money

For generations money has been the master of men. It has made war and peace; its yea and nay has thundered across the world. It has said thou shalt and thou shalt not, and men have obeyed as if it spoke with the voice of God.

Twice burned, the American people will never

be so complacent, humble and obedient regarding this man-made god. We are now watching the god's clay feet crumble. Having witnessed the senseless, unhelpful antics of its high priests, we now see their fear and confusion in the face of a disaster which "couldn't happen."

Let's begin our diagnosis with money and its place in the economic system. I assume everyone knows what money is, so I won't fill these pages with a boring tale of how it all came about: barter, Indian wampum, shark's teeth, brass earrings, Confederate bills. Nor shall I expound upon William Jennings Bryan and the free silver movement. There is one piece of historical data that I want to slip in, as follows:

BARTER MONEY POWER

Money began as a convenience. Instead of swapping a cow for a pair of goats which he didn't want, the owner of the cow accepted a disk of metal or some other acknowledged symbol of value. He took this symbol to the market and exchanged it for cloth or for something else that he really needed. That was all there was to it.

In the course of time it evolved, through a long and complicated process, into something else. It became a medium of power. Some men, seeking the advantage of wealth and influence, soon came to appreciate that control of enough money would permit control over producers and consumers.

These primitive capitalists accumulated extra money and stored it away. Accumulation was a nuisance because it meant working harder than your neighbor, being a better trader or being more miserly.

But once extra money had been put aside, its owner could exercise a distinct advantage over his neighbors. Their necessities would produce a profit for him, if he found ways to buy low and sell dear, and if he could lend his money for a fee, or what came to be called interest.

Thus did money as medium-of-exchange become money-as-power. It acquired a life and character of its own. Instead of being associated with productivity on equal terms, money took the lead. Work, the source of all human well-being, became the servant of money. And so it remains to this day.

LENDING LIMIT VS. CREDIT

When that extra money was lent, the borrower took the actual cash away with him. In those times, every shylock's lending capacity was exactly the amount of his capital—and no more. Even with high rates of interest, fortune building was slow. It took too long, and the total amount, in the end, never seemed large enough.

Then some forgotten genius conceived the idea of *fictional* money. Of course, this was probably the work of many inventors, not one. In any case, it is far and away the most ingenious device in the world of finance.

Fictional money is credit. Instead of lending actual gems, gold, silver or seashells, the lender gives a receipt, or ticket, saying the borrower has credit for renting (for a fee—interest) so many pieces of gold, silver or shark's teeth, which remain in the lender's possession. With this development the lender can lend when he has no money, and the borrower can spend money which therefore doesn't exist. The lender can do this a second, third, fourth and fifth time as long as he knows the receivers of these credit tickets will not come to him all at once demanding actual money. In fact, probably none will ever come. This made the lender's treasure-box receipt "as good as gold."

There is nothing fundamentally unsound or inherently wrong about the idea of fictional money. It is simply a form of credit expansion. Rightly used, it gives buoyancy to a nation's economic life and speeds it up. It creates a flexible and elastic currency. But it is danger-ous when mishandled. It is like strychnine, which may be a beneficent remedy in small doses, but in large doses is a ticket to the undertaker.

Unfortunately, credit invites mishandling. And that crucial weakness of credit during the course of capitalism's evolution came to be connected with a kind of romanticism. Swashbuckling cap-tains of industry competed, using credit, for monopoly positions of power. Money ceased to be a symbol of positions of value exchanged and came to be cherished as a full-blooded eco-nomic entity in itself. Removed from its origi-nal role and further weakened by credit abuses, it is now only a caricature of its real self.

Banks Create "Money"

Money is the enabler of capitalism. But capitalism's foundation should, and does, rest on men, machinery and materials. The enabling element should not control the foundation. Money should be controlled by the industrial foundation it serves. So the question arises, how can there be more bank deposits than there is money?

Most of the deposits in banks consist of credit fictions. They are created in the course of making loans. When a businessman, or anyone else, borrows money from a bank, he doesn't walk around to the teller's window and draw out the entire amount in cash—not one time in a thousand. Chances are, he won't draw out any of it in real money.

In carrying out the formalities of the loan, the bank simply makes two entries in its records. The amount the borrower has obtained is charged against him on a loan register; that's one entry. The other is the crediting of this amount to the borrower's account as a deposit.

Suppose $20,000 is borrowed. The bank's financial statement made at the end of the day's business shows a $20,000 increase in deposits, even though no money at all has been put into the bank by the borrower.

Now, here is the most important part of the transaction: the bank gives the borrower a checkbook with a lot of blank checks in it. This is, in effect, a license to issue private money on his own account up to a limit of $20,000. Thus the borrower becomes a kind of mint.

FICTIONAL MONEY—SAFETY IN GOOD TIMES

But the money the borrower dispenses is fictional; it doesn't exist. The bank does not expect to pay these checks in cash, though it will give up the cash readily enough when the check is presented. The deposit entered in the borrower's credit account is a fiction, and the checks represent a credit. Experience has shown that in normal times this kind of fictional money can be used in quantities without danger to the economic structure. Since the majority of loans made by banks extract no real money from the bank, they involve nothing more hazardous than a possible mistake in bookkeeping. They are granted to borrowers, used and paid off, without costing the bank anything. This is made possible by the highly practical device of bankers' clearinghouses.

Once a day the representatives of all the banks in the community get together and figure up what each bank owes the others. You have an account, let's say, at the Eastern Bank, but you have given checks to people who have deposited your checks in their respective banks. Next day, officials of these two banks appear at the clearinghouse with the checks, and the Eastern Bank would have to pay them in cash if it did not have in its possession checks issued by depositors of Western and Northern. So they add up the totals and usually there is a small difference in one bank's favor, and this is then paid.

That's why the total cash amount of deposits in U.S. banks is so many times more than the actual cash in circulation. Huge numbers are added and subtracted while very little cash ever moves.

BANK RESERVES

There is a limit to a bank's power to create fictional money. Every bank is required by law to hold a cash reserve which must bear a certain percentage relationship to its deposits. The reserve requirements vary according to whether the bank belongs to the Federal Reserve system or is organized under the laws of one of the states. But for the purposes of this discussion, the legal reserves may be said to run between 7% and 13% of the bank's deposits—or about 10% on the average. This means that for every dollar in cash that it possesses, the average bank may lend about ten dollars. And, of course, this ten dollars loaned becomes ten dollars deposited at the same time. But that's not all.

FEDERAL RESERVE OPERATION

In the background of this financial activity are the Federal Reserve banks, the final resource of both good and bad banking. A bank which is a member of the Fed may rediscount (or sell) its customers' IOUs to the Federal Reserve Bank in its district, provided these obligations (or promissory notes) are based on commercial or agricultural transactions.

For example; A.B. & Co., a mercantile concern, borrows $10,000 from its local bank. The collateral consists of bills for goods which A.B. & Co. sold to its customers. The bank goes through its usual procedure; it credits A.B. & Co. with $10,000 of fictional money. Against this deposit, it holds a cash reserve of, say, one or two thousand dollars. Let's assume the bank has loaned almost all of its funds, its deposits. Legally it can't lend its cash reserves. Since there is a continuing demand for loans in its community, the bank turns to the Federal Reserve.

It sends A.B. & Co.'s promissory note to the nearest Federal Reserve Bank and asks for a rediscount. The Federal Reserve grants the rediscount which means that it makes a loan of $10,000 to the local bank. Instead of sending the local bank $10,000 in Federal Reserve paper money, its deposit account in the Federal Reserve Bank is increased by $10,000. This augments the loan resources of the local bank and it can make more loans. But it hasn't the free use of the entire $10,000. The law requires that a certain percentage of deposits must be held by the Federal Reserve Bank.

The important part—in relation to the borrowing public—is that for every $1,000 credited to the local bank by the Federal Reserve, the local bank can make fresh loans of $10,000 to its customers. Ten to one. You understand, of course, that all these transactions are self-liquidating, and the loans from the Fed to member banks run for short periods. Otherwise, there would be a gigantic piling up of local bank IOUs at the Federal Reserve Banks all across the country. The process is not static but fluid. As the local bank pays off its loans at the Fed, it keeps sending on new paper for rediscount; that is, if it is in need of funds.

FRACTIONAL RESERVE BANKING EQUALS PYRAMID, POINT-DOWN

The theory behind the Federal Reserve system is that in times of healthy business expansion, credit should also expand. The member banks are not expected—and not permitted—to lean too heavily on the Federal Reserve. They are expected, at times, to clear up all their obligations. That's the theory.

The principal feature of these banking operations is that the credit structure becomes an inverted pyramid, one standing on its apex.

Bigger and bigger layers of credit are piled on top of one another. It takes wisdom and foresight of the highest order to manage these delicately balanced, inherently unstable financial structures. If something goes wrong, a domino effect causes the entire pyramid to collapse.

CHAPTER 7

DOES THE
FEDERAL RESERVE
CONTROL THE MONEY SUPPLY?

Die-Hard Ideas

We all have a vested interest in our ideas, and the last thing we want to do is change them since, as I have noted, change is an ordeal, a hardship. One mainstream idea with nine lives is that the Federal Reserve controls the money supply and interest rates. I have earlier given chapter and verse of why this is not so.

Still, as late as July 1987, two top Reagan Administration members were still trying to revive that sacred cow. The *Los Angeles Times* reported on July 1, 1987 that Beryl W. Sprinkel, the White House's chief economic advisor, warned a congressional committee, "If the slowdown in the growth of the money supply continued for several more quarters, it could put the continuation of growth and real output and employment at risk."

These remarks were echoed by former Commerce Secretary Malcolm Baldridge, who said, "Tight credit conditions would limit economic growth that has been projected at 3% to 4% over the next several months."

The story continued, saying, "The Fed had squeezed the money supply slightly in April." And so it goes. The media misreporting the data and thereby etching it deeper into the minds of the readers, not only of the *Los Angeles Times*, but other media as well. Walter Bagehot, founder of *Economist* magazine, warned in 1850 of the failure of "literary men" to report business and economic news accurately. So we are filling the circle—again.

THE MARCH OF FOLLY ROLLS ON

A February 15, 1988, *Business Week* article dealing with the Federal Reserve control of the money supply, said, "In an unusual letter to members of the Federal Open Market Committee, Assistant Treasury Secretary Michael R. Darby warned recently that continuing last year's slow growth of the money supply could imperil the economy."[1] The grasp on men's minds of economic myths seems almost mystical.

And the *Wall Street Journal*, on February 8, 1988, stated, "The Fed's policy arm meets this week to decide whether to bolster the slowing economy with lower interest rates. Irwin I. Kellner, Chief Economist, Manufacturer's Hanover Trust Company said, 'It is going to be one of the most critical policy meetings in recent memory.' The Fed appears to have loosened credit slightly, but Fed officials worry that easing too much could hurt the dollar and worsen the trade deficit."[2]

This was not only an exercise in futility, but reminds me, as baseball legend Casey Stengel once said, "It's difficult to make predictions, especially about the future."

To understand the tools used by the Fed, it is necessary to dig a little into our economic history. When the Federal Reserve Act was passed in 1913, provision was made for the Fed to perform open-market operations, i.e., to buy and sell government securities. A tool for direct control gave the Fed authority to impose a reserve requirement on member banks—25% at the start. It followed that if the Fed raised the requirement to 35% there would be a reduction in the amount of credit which banks could extend. Conversely, for the Fed to decrease the reserve requirement, it would indicate more bank credit was available. These credit-control tools provided seventy years ago continued to manipulate bank policy into the 1980s.

Curiously, it was not until 1929 that the Federal Reserve, by chance, linked open-market operations to reserve requirements as another means of controlling credit. Benjamin Strong stated in 1932 that the Federal Reserve Bank of New York discovered, partly by accident, how open-market operations in buying and selling Treasury issues could be an instrument of credit control. Since this unusual start in 1929, the Fed has used this technique deliberately and consistently to control reserve requirements.

But a question remains: Does controlling the amount of reserves actually control the money supply? The answer is "No!" Reserves are the base for credit expansion, but they are not credit expansion itself anymore than a fallen pine cone is a pine tree.

Credit expansion occurs when (1) the private sector creates loans which usually become immediately spendable deposits, and (2) banks purchase U.S. Treasury obligations. In either case, credit is generated by the banks and the public, which accounts for most of our money supply.

Reserves, Not Guarantees

Reserves were seen as a way to provide an emergency cushion against possible future bank runs. Do reserves provide complete protection? Obviously not. Even the Federal Reserve, in a candid moment, acknowledged in its *Bulletin* of November 1936 that "it became evident that reserves alone were not an adequate protection to banks and depositors."[3] That truth will be amply demonstrated in the impending crisis leading to Great Depression II. Reserve requirements have had negligible benefit to banks and the banking public.

In 1896, before incorporation of the Federal Reserve system, bank reserves were 25%. Before the crash of 1987, they were officially 12%. The following chart shows the official reserve breakdown as reported by the *Federal Reserve Bulletin* of December 1986.

Small banks, time deposits and nonpersonal time deposits require a much lower reserve of 3%. *The Federal Reserve Bulletin* of December 1986 gives this data on bank deposits.

Table 1: The Reserve Requirements of Depository Institutions, Percent of Deposits

Type of deposit and deposit interval	Member bank requirements before implementation of the Monetary Control Act		Type of deposit and deposit interval	Depository institution requirement after implementation of the Monetary Control Act	
	Percent	Effective date		Percent	Effective date
Net demand			*Net transaction accounts*		
$0 million-$2 million	7	12/30/76	$0-$31.7 million	3	12/31/85
$2 million-$10 million	9-1/2	12/30/76	Over $31.7 million	12	12/31/85
$10 million-$100 million	11-1/4	12/30/76			
$100 million-$400 million	12-1/4	12/30/76	*Nonpersonal time deposits*		
Over $400 million	16-1/4	12/30/76	By Original maturity		
			Less than 1-1/2 years	3	10/06/83
Time and savings			1-1/2 years or more	0	10/06/83
Savings	3	3/16/67			
			Eurocurrency liabilities		
Time			All types	3	11/13/80
50-55 million, by maturity					
30-179 days	3	3/16/67			
180 days to 4 years	2-1/2	1/08/76			
4 years or more	1	10/30/75			
Over 55 million, by maturity					
30-179 days	6	12/12/74			
180 days to 4 years	2-1/2	1/08/76			
4 years or more	1	10/30/75			

Table 2

	July 1986
Deposits	$1.8 trillion
Transactions deposits	539 billion
Savings deposits	490 billion
Time deposits	786 billion
Borrowings	380 billion
Other Liabilities	170 billion
Residual (assets less liabilities)	169 billion

Transactional deposits (demand deposits) totaled $539 billion. Twelve percent (12%) of that sum is $64 billion. Savings and time deposits totaled $1.276 trillion. A 3% reserve of that is $38.2 billion. Total deposits of $1.815 trillion thus require a total reserve of $102 billion. The

Federal Reserve alters that small base on a weekly basis with additions and subtractions. Conventional economic and banking theory has it that small changes in reserves make possible large changes in reserves. Perhaps when M1 was 45% of all deposits in 1960 (see Table 5), or before 1975 this was true, but when the private sector began creating so many private credit instruments and private credit that control vanished.

This is because too much credit is created by the private sector, entirely free of Federal Reserve control. Perhaps in the beginning of the Fed in 1913, it was believed that if the Fed raised or lowered reserve requirements in big numbers (up or down 30%, for example) this would impact the banks. Of course, that was generations ago, before computers and world banking. Now if the Fed gets too tough with reserve requirements, the banks simply go into the Eurocurrency market to borrow with no reserve requirements.

Obviously, prevailing banking theory is now irrelevant. We have a system where the private credit-creating sector wags the dog of publicly created credit. Remember: the Fed can only increase or decrease bank reserves. The bona fide money supply is bank loans, and the Fed is powerless to control them. If the Fed gets tough, banks flee the domestic banking system. Thus, bank credit remains out of control, in private hands, and a financial nuclear bomb has been created.

Nonreservables

After 1960 there was an astounding growth in managed liabilities—also called "nonreservables." These were credit instruments generated in the private sector to meet expanding credit needs. They were traded in various financial markets with minimal or no reserves required. Item 3 in the following table compares their growth in just six years:

Table 3: The Boom in Non-Reservables			
	1975	**1981**	**% Increase**
1. Demand deposits and other checkable deposits	$208.3	$254.2	22
2. Small-time and Large-time savings deposits	1,237.5	1,482.9	20
3. Overnight repurchase agreements; money market mutual funds; Eurodollars & commercial paper	68.9	375.9	446

Source: *Monthly Review*, December 1984, p. 12

We are all familiar with the Fed's reserve requirements in the first two categories, and with the Fed's interest rate controls. Note how the growth of these two reservable categories was stunted relative to that of Item 3. The banks were deprived of previously cheap deposits, and thus were unable to grant the usual volume of cheap loans based on such deposits.

Because these reservable sources were drying up, the banks sought other sources: overnight repurchase agreements, Eurodollars, etc. Outside the banking system, money market mutual funds, commercial paper, etc., soared as sources for corporate finance and as repositories for deposits.

Under President Reagan the process of tightening regulation was blocked, at least temporarily.

Table 4: MONEY SUBSTITUTES
Managed Liabilities—December 1985
(No Reserve Requirements)

TYPE OF INSTRUMENT	BILLIONS OF DOLLARS
Certificates of deposit	$325 estimated
Money market shares	287
Commercial paper	221
Credit cards	124
Auto Installment Loans	223
Standby letters of credit	210
Eurodollars	2,000 estimated
TOTAL CREDITS	$3,390 trillion

Source: *Statistical Abstract of the U.S., 1987*, pp. 475-476; *Federal Reserve Bulletin*, December 1986, pp. 19, 36, 116.

Money substitutes grew much faster from 1975 to 1981 than did Reservable Money, i.e., that under the control of the Federal Reserve. That uneven growth can be seen even more clearly when presented as follows:

Table 5: The Money Supply
(Average daily figures in billions)

Currency and All Types of Checking Accounts*		The Total Money Supply**	Column 1 as a % of Column 2
1960	141.8	314.3	45.1
1965	169.5	480.3	35.3
1970	216.5	674.5	32.1
1975	291.1	1161.7	25.1
1980	414.1	1936.7	21.4
1983	521.1	2599.8	20.0

*This is the sum of currency, travellers checks and all checkable deposits (which the Fed labels M1).
**This is the sum of column 1 plus savings and small-denomination time deposits at all depository institutions, overnight repurchase agreements (RP's) at commercial banks, overnight Eurodollars held by U.S. residents, money market mutual funds, large-denomination time deposits at all depository institutions and term RP's at commercial banks and savings and loan associations (which the Fed calls M3).

Source: *Monthly Review*, December 1984, p. 10

The first column presents the data for what we traditionally considered to be the basic money supply, that which the Federal Reserve originally was empowered to regulate. But the twenty-three-year growth of that basic money supply was insignificant compared with the growth of these new forms of managed liabilities. The basic money portion steadily declined from 45% in 1960 to 20% in 1983. This is a most lucid way of showing the private sector's unrestrained ability to meet its pre-crash credit needs—for whatever purpose.

The unequal growth of reservable and nonreservable reserves leads to the argument that the growth of money supply by the Fed has been materially weakened. But, it is argued, the link between the monetary base and the money stock nevertheless remains strong through the money multiplier (the ability at 12% to expand deposits eight times). However, there is no data to support this, since it merely states that there is the inherent ability to expand because of fractional reserves and that provides control.

Managed liabilities also expand similarly and with no reserve requirement. In the Eurodollar market, at least $2 trillion in size, with no reserves, the power to create credits rapidly and beyond control of any central bank is obvious.

How Powerful Is the Fed?

According to Andrew W. Caughey, a retired accounting manager at the Federal Reserve Bank of Cleveland,

"The Federal Reserve plays an important but not a decisive role in the American economy. Probably no leading institution is less understood in the public media than the Fed. In seeking simple explanations for complex phenomena, commentators consistently ascribe more influence to the Fed than it actually has. They assume that it has almost unlimited control over the money supply and that through this control, it can determine the level of interest rates, initiate a business upturn, or nip an economic recovery in the bud. Instead, the

Fed is pretty much circumscribed by the needs of the banking system.

"Was the Fed responsible for the great inflation of the past twenty-five years? The Fed can add money to the banking system by purchasing government securities in the open market. These securities become assets of the member banks, earning interest from the Treasury. When they mature, they are normally rolled over into new issues. But at the end of the year more than 90% of the interest earned on them is returned to the Treasury under the euphemism of 'Interest of F.R. Notes.' In 1983, for example, $14 billion was returned in this way. U.S. securities acquired by the Fed are, in effect, issued without payment of interest and need never by retired. They cost the Treasury almost nothing: they are 'monetized' by becoming a part of the money supply. This is the only portion of the public debt that can be likened to the *assignats* or the greenbacks of earlier times. It is not really correct to say that 'Washington inflates our currency by running the printing presses.' In reality, the federal government *borrows all of the money it needs* in excess of income—and this is a fundamental difference.

"The amount of U.S. securities held by the Fed grew from $20.8 billion in 1950 to $160.8 billion in 1983. During this same period, total U.S. securities outstanding grew from $22 billion to $1,700 billion. Total private and public debt grew from

$400 billion to over $4,000 billion. The proportion of total U.S. securities held by the Fed declined markedly. The Fed monetized $140 billion of federal debt from 1950 to 1983, an average of $4.24 billion per year. During the same period, federal budget outlays grew from $40 billion to $796 billion per year. The gross national product rose from $300 to $3,400 billion per year. And the consumer price index quadrupled. Clearly the monetizing of $140 billion, when related to these huge increases in federal outlays and the gross national product, could not have been the major factor in sustaining the inflationary process. The amount involved is simply too small.

"The real basis for the economic boom and accompanying inflation is to be found in an unprecedented expansion of private and public debt: 1000% in thirty-three years. Every resource of the federal government was utilized to spur this growth: loan guarantees, subsidized mortgage rates, low down payments, easy terms, tax credits, secondary markets, deposit insurance. The long prosperity has been built on a mountain of debt. The central influence in creating it has been the federal government. At most, the Federal Reserve System has been supportive."[4]

So much for the widely held belief the other way that the Federal Reserve prints paper money, can inflate and so on.

To recapitulate, the Federal Reserve, through a relatively small reserve requirement, was purported to control the ability of banks to lend. Proof to the contrary was found in the rapid creation of credit by the private sector to meet their own needs, bypassing the Federal Reserve system entirely where nonreservables now almost equal reservable credits in size. Of course, the banks are involved with these new instruments, but a bank's main business historically has been to make loans and expand credit.

What We Have Learned

1. The suicidal pre-crash economic expansion was fueled mainly by the growth of nonreservable credit instruments rather than by the growth of reservable money. This meant that any Fed control of reservable money, and the Fed's presumed control of the money supply, was largely irrelevant as the private sector ignored the Fed, created its own credit machine and ran it to destruction.

2. From our painful example, we might assume that economic expansion always will be financed, whether controlled or uncontrolled. If we read history carefully, we find that the answer unquestionably is yes.

3. The Federal Reserve, in addition to normal budget financing chores, had to create an additional $1 trillion per year just to

pay interest on the $11 trillion in total domestic debt. We learned that this "special" and necessary money creation had no impact whatsoever on economic growth.

4. We learned of the immense foreign policy implications which follow such private-sector credit creation. The U.S. credit dollar was still the world's reserve currency. This meant that foreign central banks could acquire dollars and, using them as a reserve base (like gold), expand their own domestic currencies. Thus the U.S. credit expansion, most of it privately executed, brought forth a world explosion in the money supply, the larger part also privately induced. Unfortunately, it was mostly squandered on pyramids which generated no new wealth. Without new wealth (useful production), that worldwide credit debt couldn't be repaid. At the end, most dollars were used to service debt. These dollars were destined to become scarce as the credit pool shrank. They became more valuable against foreign currency. The cost of borrowing them rose as their supply diminished. Their relatively high value attracted to the U.S. an excessive volume of foreign goods and investments. The U.S. became a net capital importer, and the largest debtor nation in the world. Perhaps by the time you read this, some triggering event will have pulled the plug on the steadily-shrinking credit pool: credit collapse. Proof of the im-

mense foreign policy implications of run-away credit creation.

5. Finally, we learned that the evidence strongly contradicts the conventional wisdom of monetary economists, who know that the Federal Reserve controls credit creation. By the end of 1984, use of that dead-wrong conventional wisdom reached the highest levels when the Secretary of the Treasury accused the Federal Reserve of "refusing to furnish the money supply needed for growth."

What Next?

Before the credit collapse, many solutions were proposed for rationalizing the financial system. One would have restored the gold standard. Another was Irving Fisher's "100% money." There were others. None of these attracted enough following to become policy. Perhaps history provdes the reason: when economic growth commences, it will be financed! The private sector's credit needs are always met.

We saw that proposed congressional controls to slow private sector credit growth were by-passed by the creation of still newer credit instruments. An example was the certificate of deposit, born in 1960. Again, history tells us that the U.S. economic system has always fueled recovery and growth, and the Federal Reserve Corporation cannot do much to control this process. We must remember that credit expansion is mainly a private sector function, and 79% of the pre-crash debt was there. Somehow public attention was focused on the 21% of the debt that was federal. Also, compound interest was, and still is, crucial. But compound interest, like total domestic debt and total interest burden, was ignored in public discussions. Instead the media invited us to worry about interest on the federal debt, which was roughly one-fifth of total domestic interest payments.

Always, and especially now, the government's short-run fiscal and monetary policies can produce a mass psychological impact. But in the long run, in stable times, in this extraordinarily complex society, it is not plausible that these federal maneuvers are all that important. And there is no statistical proof, over long periods, that the effect of those twin policies was ever crucial.

CHAPTER 8

THE DILEMMA
OF THE
MODEL BUILDERS

Economics by Computer

For a generation now, our economists have been under the sway of mathematics, particularly the mathematics of statistics. They have relied upon its demonstrations as proof of their theses. As might be expected, some asked too much of the tool. Karl Marx, for instance, tried to prove by means of statistics the inevitability of class conflict and the ideality of the communist state.

More recently, the development of the electronic computer coupled with the possibilities in calculus have given more range to the mathematical economist. In mathematical constructs called models, formulas occupy page after page. These are formulas that, in the absence of the computer, figuring by ordinary procedures would take a lifetime to solve. Properly programmed computers can now solve them almost instantaneously. It's little wonder that those who would envision the future are fascinated with the speed and data-handling capacity of programmed computers.

Hence they properly continued to ignore Ouija boards, horoscopes, the study of sun spots and even the institutions of common sense in favor of econometric models. Unfortunately, they increasingly ignored both common sense and intuition. Most of their prognostications relied upon two statistical masses. The first was the Gross National Product (GNP); the other was the money supply known heretofore as M1 or M1b.

As the second and third legs of the crash approached, consternation was thrown into their profession by two warnings authorities who had cause to doubt the reliability of the two constructs. During the past decade of volatile trade and finance, economists whose business is forecasting tomorrow's Dow Jones average or the price of gold have hung anxiously on the periodic issuance of the GNP estimate. This was published by the Department of Commerce about ten days before the end of each quarter.

But even Commerce Department officials took pains to remind all of the doubtful value of the quarterly GNP figure. The problem arises from the absence of data on the third month of the quarter (except as to inventories), and the correctness of the assumptions on which estimates for that month must rely. Below these problems, however, lies a much deeper complication that throws the entire process into doubt.

GNP purportedly reports the total output of the economy during the period. Actually, a measure of the output is statistically impossible because the raw data cannot be reported in dollars of constant value or purchasing power.

Dollar value is always changing. Even when the data is adjusted by a "deflator," the index is implicitly inaccurate, for output consists of immeasurable items; some output is reported by weight, like steel, and other by numbers, like eggs.

A deeper defect exists in that the new data measures consumption, not output, even though adjustments are made for inventories. What is reported is what people spend, not what the economy produces.

Of even greater importance to both theoreticians and entrepreneurs is not how much is produced, but what kind is produced. In recent decades a major shift has occurred in spending, from expenditures on objects that produce (so-called durable goods) to objects that are consumed. How they are consumed has become significant, but cannot be measured. Spending for prepared restaurant meals, for example, is reported in the same way as spending for basic groceries. While the actual amount of food entered into the data may be the same, it will show up as $20 in the shopping bag and $120 in the restaurant. In times of recession and depression, householders may purchase more basic foodstuffs and curtail their restaurant spending. This results in a decline in GNP but no actual decline in food produced and consumed.

Fifty years ago, when GNP was being developed in the Commerce Department, the noted economist Franklin W. Ryan pointed out that the GNP omitted the greatest productive sector of the economy—the household. It was omitted because there is no monetary measure for the value of the products, from butter to babies, that the household produces.

The figures for money supply are equally deceptive. As we know, the term "money" is deceptive enough. Money supply, indicated as M1, represents the total legal tender circulating, plus so-called checkbook money, represented by instant purchasing power in the form of demand deposits in banking institutions. But what circulates is not money if one excludes the small amount of coinage in the whole. Money, since its invention in the seventh century B.C., has always and everywhere meant coinage. And this was the concept of money incorporated in the U.S. Constitution. Gold and silver coins (or their depository receipts) were the only fully legal tender until 1934.

Today the principal circulation consists of Federal Reserve notes, which are merely promises to pay—but promises without maturity and without means of redemption—issued by a private, autonomous corporation. Bank check money consists of the deposit liabilities of the banking system, some of which may be of doubtful worth, particularly if drawn on banks which may have been forced to close never to reopen and for which the FDIC (Federal Deposit Insurance Corporation) cannot cover the losses. Money supply, M1, rose and fell not in accord with the amount of currency and coin flowing into the Treasury, but with the increase or decrease in total debt.

The Federal Reserve authorities tried to regulate the amount of debt by adjusting the reserves which banks had to carry and which limited the amount of their lending. Under this system the Fed authorities could influence the increase in banking deposit liabilities (loans to account holders), but not their decrease.

The Fed can try to influence the amount of borrowing by the public—by the rate it sets on its own lending to its member banks—but the actual total is beyond its power. The total debt, or purchasing power, of the economy rests on willingness or unwillingness of individuals and institutions to borrow. Thus, despite the requirement imposed by Congress upon the Fed in 1979 to set, and to announce targets for money supply, the task eludes execution. Hence, the pre-crash dissatisfaction with the weekly M1 and other aggregate figures.

Will More Credit Bring Lower Rates of Interest?

A popular delusion, particularly on Capitol Hill, was that the Federal Reserve could lower high interest rates by increasing the money supply—namely, the amount of debt. But interest rates are a reflection of the anticipated value of the currency received at maturity of the debt. And the effect of increasing the money supply is the same as increasing the supply of any commodity: it tends to depress the price of the commodity—in the case of money, its value. An increase in M1 is more likely than not to force interest rates higher rather than lower. Lenders will want a higher interest rate to offset the lower purchasing power of money paid back by the borrower.

A collateral misconception was that the supply of credit (i.e., the amount of lending) was some fixed amount, and that large federal borrowing to meet budgetary deficits had the effect of crowding out other borrowers. That also was an error. The amount of lending power in the economy is practically limitless, if the prospect of return is present.

The amount of lending available is affected by the budget deficit only to the degree that lenders think the size of budgetary deficits affect the ability of the government to meet its obligations. We are really just beginning to ponder this now. Unwillingness of the market to lend to the government, for any reason, forces the government to use the power of the Federal Reserve, which must purchase any amount of government debt by increasing the banking system's reserves and by issuing its unneeded legal tender.

If either or both the new credit and currency are used, the value of money will decline, prices will rise, and interest rates will go up so that lenders will come out ahead of the inevitable inflation when the loan is paid off. The above, however, is only instructive, since the system has given us, or will give us, the opposite set of problems. Rather than endure inflation and rising prices, we will be forced to live with deflation and with trying to get the credit bubble out of all prices. How will we do this? Only time will tell.

CHAPTER 9

FORGOTTEN AND HIDDEN ECONOMIC HISTORY

The Future's Shadows

Economic events do not spring out of vacuums. They are formed and moved by their antecedents. Whether known to us or not, those events are the result of prior activity. In other words, the future casts its shadow.

As early as the fall of 1979, as in 1929, the mass media and America's leading economists were advising the public that another depression could not happen. According to *Business Week*, "The conventional wisdom is that the U.S. economy cannot dip lower than a mild recession. If the economy appears to be heading down, people believe that Social Security, unemployment insurance and other income-generating mechanisms will prevent starvation; the Securities Exchange Commission (SEC) and Federal Deposit Insurance Corporation (FDIC) will prevent financial disaster and a government positioned and prepared to take action will find solutions in time."[1]

Nothing could be further from the truth.

In 1929 consumers had built up their indebtedness in the heady atmosphere of that boom, only to find the value of their financial assets evaporate after the stock market crash. By 1987 consumers had built up a much larger indebtedness in installment and mortgage borrowing, over $2 trillion, nearly as much as Uncle Sam owed! The slightest triggering event could, and did, bring the U.S. economy down like a falling rock.

During the 1970s consumers increased debt, both to defeat inflation and to repay loans with cheaper dollars. But economic slowdown produced layoffs and the loss of two incomes per family. This presented consumers with a shrinking standard of living, guaranteeing they would be unable to pay off their debts. No, they didn't starve. Unemployment checks rolled in, but were debts being repaid? Those debts gained a stranglehold on the economy and led, eventually, to the inability to repay both our current and future obigations.

History, too often forgotten, shows that prolonged inflation will tempt the consumer, the corporation and the government to borrow too heavily in the struggle to keep up. When the inflation is over, cash flows sharply decline and those debts cannot be repaid. Debts simply fall of their own weight.

They did in 1929 and will again when Great Depression II hits. Buying by consumers began a sharp decline by early 1988. That meant fewer sales, less production, layoffs and a massive slowdown that could only be reinflated with additional credits, as the U.S. government has done since 1945.

It will soon be clear, if it isn't already, that the ideas of Keynes have turned on themselves and on the policymakers who followed them. For debt has continued to mount; it now stands at $11 trillion in the U.S. and an additional $2 trillion Eurodollars which the U.S. cannot honor. What went wrong?

The Hidden Shift

The problem is not a shortage of goods. That hasn't been the problem in the U.S. for many years. Gilbert Haas of New York City, a friend and shrewd observer of our present economic mess, argues that our productive capacity grew greatly from 1945 on, and that it was technology which really invited the final credit explosion which started in the 1970s. It was this vast new credit base that encouraged the masses to consume the overproduction of goods made possible by technological advances.

Production of goods was not the problem. Distribution was, and continues to be, our real unsolved problem. Unknowingly we tried to apply old "commodity money" exchange concepts in a credit money age, and wound up with a pyramid of debt which now can only be liquidated.

COMMODITY MONEY

Before mass production, mankind had been accustomed to commodity money—money which has value in itself. We had a fairly accurate knowledge of this metal, or metal-backed, money and had developed a set of laws regarding its use, all based on long experience and observation.

In the beginning we had learned to save tangible things such as food, clothing and fuel, and finally commodity money, consisting of precious metals and gems. These things were wealth. They were not credits. When we had accumulated enough of this real wealth, we prudently invested a portion in tools and materials, or bought stock in corporations. In short, we became capitalists. And this capitalistic wisdom was sound. Wealth was produced and it was saved to become capital again, increasing production (a form of wealth) still more. The world grew richer.

Then came the transition from commodity money to credit money. The move was so gradual and unheralded that mankind failed (and generally still fails) to differentiate between real wealth and this new credit instrument which so outwardly resembles money. "Think of it as money," proclaimed the old Visa credit card television commercial.

The original concept of money changed as we become more and more dependent upon modern economic systems, and almost completely dependent on corporate employment also. This dependency changed the idea of "money as commodity" to "money as credit"—a right to buy the goods, not the goods themselves. Production and exchange had depended on the old money system, which quietly transformed into a credit system. Thus, the use and control of credit became all-important to the American public, even though we didn't yet distinguish it from commodity money.

CREDIT MONEY

When money was a commodity, man saved real wealth and then invested it in real-wealth tools, which generally produced real-wealth goods. But ideas which were sound when applied to commodity money are unsound when applied to credit money because credit money possesses a radically different character.

When we began to apply these old, sound principles to saving and investing in credit money, something very different resulted. Before, men exchanged credit profits for equities in real capital and became thereby true investors and capitalists. Now, however, men purchase evidence of debt, and instead of becoming investors, become moneylenders.

In the old days men saved the capital itself (property, houses, etc., paid for), but in our time debt has become a substitute for investment so the mortgage replaces the home owned. We now exchange paper instead of the real wealth represented by real property, not claims.

Now we find ourselves on the troubled sea of a debt economy. A debt economy has no place in sound economics, and always leads to financial instability, hard times, depression.

Unspent credit accumulation and debt creation, instead of wealth production, is the result. What we produce is debt and credit. But we will soon rid ourselves of this parasitic debt economy, and we will do this involuntarily. The debts will simply self-destruct, liquidated.

We pay a terrible price for our misuse of credit because its ultimate liquidation results in curtailed production, high unemployment, wild speculation and too many on welfare and unemployment compensation. Still, *Business Week* in an entire issue devoted to "The End of the Industrial Society,"[2] described the ingenuity of our bankers and financiers in developing a new and endless array of credit instruments.

Piling Credit on Credit, Debt Adding to Debt

Business Week argues that our financial system has been operating under 1930s laws while trying to accommodate growing demand. They describe in some detail how bankers have slyly circumvented those laws, reflecting the fact that bank assets in 1979 were twenty times larger than they were in 1929. Bankers learned to get around laws by going overseas (the $2 trillion Eurodollar market being a prime example). But banks also invented the certificate of deposit, borrowing money at one rate to relend it at another rate, thus enabling them to outbid everyone else for money with abnormally high interest rates.

Attracting Lendable Money

In the old days banks used to lend (create credits) using otherwise idle money in customers' checking accounts (demand deposits). This lendable fund was called "free" money, since banks paid no interest on checking accounts. However, by 1966 banks held more savings accounts balances than no-interest demand (checking account) balances. By the fall of 1979 six dollars out of every ten dollars banks lent had to be purchased by paying interest to savings accounts.

Since then, to feed the growing tiger, banks have created many fancy instruments to attract lendable funds: NOW accounts (Negotiable Orders of Withdrawal), telephone transfer accounts, corporate savings accounts, credit union share drafts, automatic transfer accounts. Not to mention floating-rate notes, pooled savings accounts, and pooled mortgage accounts, upon all of which new credits were created either in the U.S. or in Europe. Clearly, 1930s laws could not feed the 1980s debt machine with its crushing interest demands. If the game had to be played by 1930s rules, the banks did an admirable job of bending, innovating and "puffing" to suit the voracious 1980s.

Cycles as Hidden Economic History

Three phenomena have pushed economic cycles out of our day-to-day frame of reference:

1. Economics is taught as a science on campuses. History is not so honored.

2. Popular wisdom has been sold eternal growth as the touchstone. Our perceptions are faced up and ahead to ever-bright horizons, not behind to shadowy forests.

3. The hypnosis of the marketplace has us all (as in 1928–29) eagerly watching and participating in the big show.

Thus economic cycles and history are forgotten and hidden from pubic view.

THE LONG WAVE

Long, fifty-year cycles, or waves, were discovered in the 1920s by a Russian economist, Kondratieff. Recent research at MIT seems to confirm Kondratieff's conclusions, which were based largely on intuition. His actual data was very sketchy, I believe, having read his work in its original English edition. At any rate, Dr. Jay Forrester, an electrical engineer and professor at MIT, was refining a computer model of the national economy when he discovered, by accident, an integration between the model's consumer and capital sectors, which produced violent fluctuations covering forty-five to sixty years. Remember, this is within the two-hundred-year-old history of capitalism. "The instability inherent in capitalism may have been described this depression-creating process," stated Forrester.[3]

According to Forrester, these long waves represent massive expansion of the capital sectors of the economy followed by a relatively rapid collapse in their output as markets saturate and the mature technology no longer attracts capital. This peak of activity is followed by a ten-year plateau, then a drop into depression for another ten years or so. The cycle then repeats a new 30-year climb to another peak.

A 10-Year Depression?

Forrester's argument for a mild decade of depression is based on the strange notion that we can afford a ten-year depression but no longer. He conceives that there is already enough capital (production capacity) to support current living standards for another decade, so there is no reason for the downslope of the long wave to be a time of mass poverty.

History does not support his optimism. There was plenty of capital plant in place in the 1930s, but final demand (the consumer) was not there. Now our so-called economic stabilizers like Social Security, welfare, unemployment compensation and a host of other government funding programs theoretically are supposed to maintain a viable standard of living by keeping the capital equipment working at some lower level. But low income, even with low prices, will support only a bare standard of living—a poverty-level standard. Will the public accept this unpleasant doled-out lifestyle, or will they become small farmers again, emigrate or revolt?

Rebuilding Capital

Forrester believes that a depression is required for a society to use up excess capital plant and eliminate debt. I believe, by contrast, our excess capital will be around for a very long time if the present system survives. For example, our present auto-engine plants average sixty-five years in age, having survived the Great Depression. But I think Forrester is correct about depression's elimination of debt. That's as sure as death and taxes.

He also estimates that it takes thirty years to rebuild capital on a new or modified technological base. Each thirty-year period provides a unique cluster of technologies. Looking back, we find these examples:

1. In transportation, it was canals, then railroads and now aircraft, with the automobilization of America perhaps the biggest technological change of all; it took place in two phases—the 1920s and the post-World War II years.

2. In energy, there was a wood-burning phase, then coal burning and finally an oil-burning phase.

Forrester thought our corporations unsuited to survive the next depression. I would agree, since many of them will be liquidated by the debts they have incurred. In addition, Forrester felt that our corporations are too large, inhibiting the competition needed to establish a new technological base. Building that new base would be aided by bankruptcies which normally wipe out old managements and shake an economic system into a new shape.

Again I would agree with Dr. Forrester that bankruptcies will crumble conglomerates into smaller, highly competitive, innovative firms. They, and brand new companies, will create a new technological base, which will attract lenders and capital to generate the next thirty-year expansion in Kondratieff's long cycles.

Public enchantment with large corporations has waned during the last few years. Those that already have closed their doors or have been broken up are serving as scapegoats in the public mind. Multinational commercial banks in particular are the victims of this spiteful attitude; much public confidence was created and betrayed by these banks as they designed and hyped the "hot money" funds.

CAPITAL WITHOUT LABOR

We have been told that inflation raised the cost of corporate borrowing during the 1970s as industry moved from being capital-intensive to labor-intensive, because labor is cheaper. Is that true? As a general statement, it is false. The post-World War II baby boom created a 1970s labor pool that was absorbed in mindless, dead-end service sector jobs at McDonald's, Burger King and Taco Bell. Automation, runaway shops and cheap imports killed the industrial sector demand for the eighteen-year-old workers of the baby boom.

Production firms borrowed, despite the interest burden, not to hire young workers but to buy new technology with which they could produce more goods cheaper, with less labor than ever before in history. The final result is that producing goods is no longer a problem. Finding jobs is. Capital (production in factories) no longer depends on assembly line workers. Capital, producing at an output level to satisfy reduced depression demand, will continue. But the hands that did not produce the goods hold no money with which to buy them. To what productive purposes can these hands, and minds, be put? Can restoration of the nation's ecological equilibrium be made labor-intensive through a new and larger Civilian Conservation Corps? Certain anarchy or Watts-type riots are not useful.

AFTER THE FORTY-YEAR BINGE

I have argued that the rise in our standard of living from 1945 to 1987 has been a curiosity of economic history. In most countries of the world, living standards for the average person have been quite low, and have remained so for centuries. This recent American living-standard binge was exactly that, and not a forerunner of the future. When it is buried, it may never rise again.

Most of us who have felt uneasy with the plastic, frenetic lifestyle will have little lasting trauma when returning to the gentler mode which better suits mankind's nature. Within all nature there is balance and rhythm. It is only people, Americans and their clones, who are out of nature's balance and rhythm. When the crash deepens, balance will be forced upon us. Whoever accepts it will survive the transition, the violent responses to the cessation of normal, and vital, services.

Social unrest will be moderated by government intervention and by our own adjustment to a new, and more honest, reality. The ability of humans to make life-sustaining adaptations is one of the major lessons of history and human behavior. While we'll see this ability misused as many adapt to savage, subhuman grubbing, we cannot deny this desire which spurs the fittest to survive.

Rebellions usually have short lives, are unsuccessful and have minor lasting effects. We obviously have some of the important ingredients for revolution, but the important components to provide sufficiency are missing. The odds are very much against organized unrest in the near future. Following the critical first shock of an earthquake, aftershocks diminish in intensity. Events following this economic and social earthquake will do likewise, and we will return to what we will come to see as normal in a new and diminished reality.

Signs of an Era's End

Unmistakable signs that the old era is ending were written all around us by the middle 1980s. But those whose minds were locked into the status quo could not read those signs. And they were not alone, for neither could the citizens of other industrialized nations, and the era was ending for them also. The signs:

1. An evergrowing debt load, propelled by compounded interest.

2. Government financing became increasingly difficult.

3. The buying power of the public approached zero, eaten up by inflation, taxes, rising debts, installment and mortgage interest.

4. As buying power vanished, fewer mass-produced items could be sold domestically.

5. Selling that overproduction abroad was far from certain. Again, shrinking buying power, plus exchange rates, protectionism and quotas take their toll.

6. Growing expenditures for the military establishment. The U.S. has spent more than $1 trillion since Ronald Reagan became President. All these expenditures are supported by heavy taxes on the consuming public, which, as noted, was already less able to pay.

7. Resistance to change. Old school capitalists still among us worked overtime mindlessly maintaining their outmoded economic status. For example, after years of slow growth topped with inflation and accompanied by sluggish productivity gains and capital investment we were told that it was *supply* that must be stimulated rather than *demand.*

This last was another adventure into Wonderland, where Alice would explain what is called supply-side economics. If the stock market Crash of October 19, 1987, had not happened, another generation of economists would be busy asking and responding to senseless questions while ignoring our basic problems.

There was no rationality to supply-side economics, but the status quo economists continued working on this theory. They believed that they could find the answers, and then lo and behold, we would be on our way again, into another round of more of the same, bigger is better, ad nauseum!

8. Finally, there was the clear indication that control over credit, both public and private, had been lost. Both Westernized and developing nations abused a normally useful credit system. In the U.S., citizens clamored to convert savings into restricted interest-bearing credits. The collective debt so developed grew almost infinitely. It could do nothing else but collapse, destroying the system.

How could such inherent abuses have occurred among supposedly rational, civilized people? Thorstein Veblen wrote, in *Theory of The Leisure Class*, "Wherever the institution of private property is found, even in the slightly developed form, the economic process bears the character of a struggle between men for the possession of goods. Freedom from scruple, from sympathy, honesty and a regard for life may, within wide limits, be said to further the success of the individual in the pecuniary culture."[4]

What that spells is *greed*, which joins with its companion *fear of loss* to create social chaos.

A SOBERING NOTE ON
SUPPLY-SIDE THEORY

The crucial weakness in our capitalistic structure was certainly not what our pre-crash economic experts claimed, i.e., produce more goods by increasing industrial capacity. Note this chart:

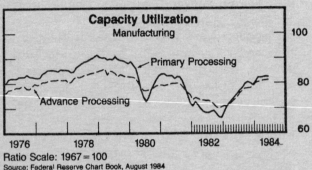

Ratio Scale: 1967 = 100
Source: Federal Reserve Chart Book, August 1984

You can plainly see we are not close to 100% capacity from 1950 through late 1984. This is a rough measure, but the producing of goods in America is not the problem. The problem is distributing goods. It's obvious, then, that constraints on the economy in the post-crash period will have nothing to do with increasing plants and equipment.

Money Is Not Capital

As might be expected, even after the crash, control of our money and credit system will be allowed to remain in private hands. Ownership and control still demands its reward. Interest is a privately-decreed reward for the use of buying power, comprised of money or credit, or other instruments.

Interest is the rental price for money. It is the rent that producers, distributors, consumers and others who need buying power must pay to those who control money for the privilege of easily exchanging their goods and labor. Barter is always more complicated.

This arbitrary interest is a ransom paid by borrowers to realize values they already own. Under this financial system, enterprise and labor are heavily taxed for the privilege of producing and exchanging goods by those who control the money structure.

Money is not capital. It is a separate and all-important facilitating factor in the production of wealth. Barter is not as handy, although computerized exchanges have eased that problem recently. After a crash, as production declines or ceases, the income to all parties in the system largely shrinks or ceases. Creditors can for a time force an income return in money, but this flow of buying power to creditors rapidly disappears unless production is resumed. Debtors can't repay creditors unless goods and services are produced and sold.

Our giant physical capacity has always been able to produce and distribute several times the volume of wealth we ever created and sold before the crash. It is finance that is the problem.

It will continue to be the problem in the future unless that system, once its flaws have been exposed, is sharply revised.

HIGHER RATES, LOW BORROWING?

Did the Fed's increase in interest rates actually reduce the number of loans and investments? Despite all the popular expectations and hoopla to make us believe this idea, the Fed's own data says No! The reason was simple: consumers, except in the purchase of a house, ignored the interest they paid on whatever they bought, including autos (Visa charging 18% was a prime example). Businessmen paid whatever rate they had to pay for financing inventories during inflation in order to stay in business. They simply passed on the price of borrowed money in higher prices for their goods and services. So the theory that the Fed could control the amount of lending was just so much hokum.

The Fed confidently asserted, and most people believed, that its manipulations could control the money supply. The bottom line is, if they'd been sincere, they could have. If the Fed had increased reserves (which banks must hold against deposits) from the 1984 average of 6% to 50%, business would have ground to a halt. Instead they fed the system, steadily increasing amounts of credit over a very long time span, and gulled a generation of workers from 1945 to 1979. This steady infusion of bank credit money guaranteed that there was enough credit for business to finance still more business, so as to always be growing.

CONTROLLING CREDIT

Proposals were frequently made that credit be allowed to grow commensurate with growth rates in production, at an average, say of 4% per year, thus always providing enough grease for the wheels of production. Again we return to the shrewdness and creativeness of credit users in expanding the original credit many times by inventing and employing many additional credit instruments well beyond the control of the Federal Reserve or anyone else.

Examples: Corporate IOUs (commercial paper), $227 billion worth; the $2 trillion Eurodollar market; $1.9 trillion in mortgage loans.[5]

What can we espouse after the impending crash to prevent another credit collapse? If we retain industrial capitalism, will the financial system have to be nationalized? Wouldn't that be another bureaucratic monster?

We created agencies to take care of the aged, the unemployed, the indigent, the handicapped, etc. Can the same be done to control credit? Should we feed our credit system a strong dose of government-control medicine? I think not, because the runaway credit creation we have now (on a global level it's more than $15 trillion) is never going to be fully repaid. Ever! It would not be helpful to have our government caught up in more debt than it manages to accumulate on its own.

Historic Economic Truisms

Economists, generally, have failed to give human behavior its proper weight in their analyses. Human behavior data-gathering is limited to consumer sentiment surveys. But they are rigged, and quite inaccurate. People think and behave today as they did when Noah's Ark was built. As econometricians move offstage, human behavior must be given a stronger place in our economic concepts and planning.

There are certain economic truisms:

1. The distribution of income remains the same within a narrow range, in all times and in all societies. A. C. Pigou, a famed old style historical economist discovered this. And it's still true.

2. The hoary concept of "bigger is better" obviously is still failing in execution. The history of capitalism is the history of this growth idea, based on the simple and reasonable notion that if we grow, producing more, then more people will be benefited with material goods. This worthy concept coupled with the irresponsible execution has brought us, again, to the brink of great human misery. And all because growth was pulled into a financial trap sprung by uncontrolled greed rather than being paced by the production of real wealth.

Simply put, our economic growth was artificial, financed by runaway credit to a point beyond the system's ability to repay the debt. Unfortunately, debt and its interest must be repaid, either by the borrower or the lender. As a large grower of tomatoes, quoted by the *Los Angeles Times*, said, "I started this business with 67 cents and now, in the true American tradition, I'm a million dollars in debt."

This is the root of the system: credit finance. "Them that has, gets," as the cliche goes. And it is this deeply-ingrained credit philosophy in all of us, especially our youth, that must be minimized if we are to survive at least, and at best to avoid repeating this calamity.

Solutions for the U.S.

1. We must put the wholesaling of credit under national control, and the retailing of credit (lending) under local control. The same is true for energy. These are central planks for the future, if we are to have one. Of course, mistakes will be made and bankers and oilmen will deplore the whole idea. But we can't afford their mistakes again, and national control of credit expansion may limit cyclical crises.

2. We must encourage redevelopment of labor-intensive industries to share national output with our capital-intensive, robotized factories. Some mix, measured against humanized criteria, will allow engineers to

apply their precious technology. Complementing that technology will be factory workers previously locked out by their capitalist employers. We might put an end to exporting our textile, steel and other industries. That would imply massive changes in the way we have done things, especially our past run-away-from-labor philosophies.

3. We have large government in our society because the masses have been taught to demand it, like it or not. Pruning governmental bureaucracy is not likely if we are to hold together some semblance of social cohesion and public pride. History has never been free of bureaucratic mandarins. Perhaps we can hope for their greater efficiency and effectiveness without tyranny.

4. Although we are already far along, we must continue converting from a production society to a service society, since all of our goods can be produced easily in large factories by computers and robots. This change is only now reaching public consciousness. We are still possessed with the ideas of the past—the growth production goals of old capitalism, including railroads, canals, autos, nuclear energy and so on, while ignoring and/or under-capitalizing our service sector. It has employed most workers, many unskilled, along with the highly educated, in running our new "overhead society." For equal capital costs, service is even more profitable than growth produc-

tion. We must adjust public thinking to this major change already happening in America. History confirms that people spend for services just as they do for goods.

Many believe this trend to services to be a dead end. For example, the late Gilbert Haas, a Wall Street money manager, wrote about this to his clients, "To simplify the implications of these trends [from production to services] it is as if two entrepreneurs—by taking in each other's washing at increased volume and price—suffer a delusion, not unlike the one afflicting most of today's leading economists, that they are enjoying a healthy business expansion, unaware of the reality that they're running out of soap."[6]

Unfortunately, the trend seems to be irreversible, and it is spreading to other advanced industrial nations such as Japan, Germany, etc.

CHAPTER 10

THE ECONOMY WORKS DIFFERENTLY THAN YOU THINK

GNP Isn't All We Buy

In the U.S. the media encourage us to think only of the current growth or decline of the Gross National Product (GNP). GNP is defined as the total value of goods and services produced in a given period. In the fourth quarter of 1986, for example, annual GNP was running about $4 trillion in current dollars. We are taught that this $4 trillion was the total supply of real value on which to spend our money during this period of time. We were misled.

The figure is far from representing the entire supply of real values available for money purchase. To assume so is to disregard all of the existing capital wealth of the nation. A person with money in hand and a decision to spend has two principal targets at which to aim. One, and only one, consists of current goods produced and services rendered as counted in GNP.

Real and Paper Property

The second target is all existing property, including land and buildings, used goods, productive plant and equipment, plus an enormous pile of paper property (debt), such as stocks, bonds, mortgages, savings accounts, checking accounts, money market fund accounts, insurance and pension assets (more debt), commercial paper, certificates of deposit, Eurodollar deposits, etc.

This second category of values lies entirely outside the national product (GNP) and corresponds to the national wealth. This money wealth (capital assets) is generally thought of as investments.

$5 AND $20 TRILLION

Money wealth (which is debt) was, in the fourth quarter of 1986, $11 trillion; it is better called "visible debt." It is interesting to note that only 21% of this total represented federal government debt, about which we hear so much. Nor did it include Eurodollar debt of almost $2 trillion. The combined totals are almost triple that of the heralded goods producing center (GNP). Also, when capital assets already bought and paid for are included, their total runs into perhaps $20 trillion—a conservative guess. GNP is merely the tip of a giant iceberg, yet it captures our total attention via media-imposed perceptions of what the American economy is and how it functions.

Fuzzing the Figures

The sale of capital assets obviously requires the same quantity of money to serve as its medium of exchange as does the sale of an equal volume of national product (GNP). As a result, at any given time, some part of the total money supply is employed in national product transactions and the other larger part is employed in capital asset transactions.

Therefore, there are at all times two distinct money supplies and two distinct velocities of money, which is an indicator of how fast it goes from one source to another.

The first pair is in the market for national product (GNP), and the second pair in the market for money wealth (our debts). Combining the total money supply serving both markets and relating it to only one market (GNP) is meaningless. Yet this is standard procedure.

How fast money changes hands (velocity) in one market is not related to the rate at which money turns over in the other market. But they are lumped together, obscuring the real dynamics.

LAW OF PRICES

Each of the two separate markets must stand separately, according to the law of prices—a supply-demand relationship where prices rise as demand rises and vice versa.

The price level in each market must be higher as the quantity of velocity of money in each market rises, and lower as the supply of values in each market rises. But there is no dam between the markets other than the habits of people, and these change. Thus the amount of money used and the price of values in each market constantly changes on its own behalf, and relative to the other.

This means that the two markets jointly must also comply with the law of prices as an aggregate, as well as separately. As demand for money moves from the GNP market to the national wealth market, prices must go down in the first and up in the second, and vice versa when demand moves from national wealth back to the GNP market.

Remember that the GNP was a $4 trillion market, and currently money wealth (which is visible debt outstanding) was an $11 trillion market. Other paid-for-capital assets equal at least $20 trillion. Of the money used in both markets, we should have been concerned with that part which was credit money (debt). Of course, the proportion of credit money was far higher in the national wealth market, where constant refinancing means the credit-money portion always grows. Unfortunately, that growth was generally ignored in our disoriented conventional wisdom. Instead, we were being focused on a poorly defined and counted abstraction called GNP growth.

GNP—Money-Wealth Imbalance

In our hypnotic fixation on the enormous money-wealth sector, we seemed almost deliberately to weaken the goods-production sector. In that atmosphere, who would have thought of its revitalization?

Supply-side economic thinking would create incentives for business to increase production. But businessmen could not be bribed or cajoled into investing in expanding production when robotics technology had already done that job for them. When supply-side tax breaks were bestowed upon pre-crash businessmen, they moved funds, in their quest for profits, to the larger sector, the money-wealth sector, making it still larger by investing their tax proceeds in high-yield T-bills. The talk of a capital shortage was nonsense, and effectively camouflaged the mistaken attempt to revive a dying sector with public tax breaks.

For debt to expand, there must be a net increase in its growth. If you borrow to repay a loan, there is no increase. And when a loan is paid off, it disappears for no increase.

Where does a net increase in debt come from? It comes from borrowing—from making a new loan that never before existed on the bank's books.

You use the proceeds for any purpose you want. The effect is a net increase in your debt, and a net increase in all of the debt outstanding in the U.S. Thus the supply of debt money (money wealth) is increased. This normally would cause the interest rate to fall, since the debt supply would be greater than demand.

In pre-crash capitalism, remember, most current visible debt was not used to produce real wealth. It was siphoned off into the other, larger money-wealth sector, making money wealth instead of goods and services.

What we called inflation was, in fact a large increase in the level of debt, money wealth, aided by interest compounding. And that increase in money wealth (debt) is one key to inflationary prosperity by the process of inflation. Prosperity is greater when there is a large body of money wealth to be taxed. In the U.S. that requirement was easily met, and huge "prosperity" resulted.

SIX PERCENT (6%) "USURY"

Over long periods of history, mankind has been able to increase the production of goods about 3.5% per year. In those same long periods, debt has increased at about the same rate. When, in biblical times, an interest rate of 6% was charged, it was called "usury" because the lender was literally "using" the borrower by demanding more interest for the money than could be produced to repay it. But in our modern era, debt (money wealth) has increased geometrically while the production of goods has increased arithmetically.

This happens in an advanced industrialized society where interest compounds. Then debt income alone adds an extra thrust to the lender's growing income, so his rewards are greater for producing debt than for producing goods.

Ultimately, however, it all self-destructs, since so much of the debt income is siphoned off from the GNP sector which produces goods, the only real source of real wealth. There are not enough goods and services produced to pay the interest costs. The paper money wealth sector then collapses, dragging down everything, as has happened many times before in America.

COMPUTERS AND PARASITES

Dr. Wesley Mitchell, an early respected American economist, noted that the driving force of capitalism is the quest for profit. World War II gave U.S. producers of goods a quantum leap in production technology. And those war-born capabilities have continued to accelerate until we can make more goods than our masses can consume. Those capabilities finally reached the point where manufactured goods (industrial society) became less profitable than their distribution and sale (on credit), which ballooned consumer debt.

Debt growth, in turn, was accelerated by the computer, which made possible the tremendous expansion of credit at low cost and high profit. It facilitated interest compounding, which encouraged the creation of countless financial parasites.

Resulting high-interest investment programs focused the attention of too many Americans on the quest for profit. Few realized that their money was in the paper-wealth sector, which, like all parasites, will ultimately destroy its life-giving host, in this case the real-wealth sector.

Hopefully, America's twenty-year shift out of the industrial society and into the paper-debt society will not become a case of accidental suicide.

INTEREST ISN'T RENT

When we see interest, we know money wealth is present. The two are inevitably linked, usually in terms of money. Interest is the periodic income, also fixed in terms of money, that is payable to the lender of money wealth. The right to receive this periodic income is what gives money wealth its value, and distinguishes it from mere money, which has no value. It is sometimes said that interest is the rental price of money. Earlier I used this reference, "rented," in keeping with the conventional wisdom. But it's a serious error to confuse the literal meanings of interest and rent.

According to the law of supply and demand, if interest were the price of money, rates must go down as the supply of money goes up. The Keynesian objective of low interest rates could then be achieved by monetary inflation. Alas, the idea is false.

Interest isn't really the price of money, any more than a motorcycle is the price of the money which buys it. Money, having no value in and of itself, has no price of its own. Money is the price of other things of value.

In the moneylending process, it is interest—or more specifically, the money-contract which bears interest—that is the subject of negotiation, not the money itself. It is the interest that is being bought by the money loaned, not the money which is being rented for the interest.

A borrower does not rent money, in the usual sense of keeping it and returning it later. He sells his own contract to pay interest now and principal later, and he quickly buys something else with the money he receives for selling for contract.

The point is not, in the slightest, merely academic. If interest were the price of money, interest would be as universal as money. In that case, it might have something like the importance that is usually attached to it by economics and finance.

In reality, interest is merely the market price prevailing in but one of the markets of commerce, the market for debt—for bonds and credit and other interest contracts. And this is the market which has become so tremendous in the U.S.

CHAPTER 11

IMPORTANT
ECONOMIC LAWS

Charles Gudie, a renowned French historian, wrote: "The economic world, like the physical world, has its laws. We may misunderstand them, but we cannot escape them. Sometimes they act with us, and sometimes against us. They please us, but they never consider us. It is for us to please them."

How are we to find out about these laws since they are not codified like divorce, corporate, criminal or civil laws? They are, rather, concepts and ideas, and each circumstance tends to lend a new interpretation or evaluation to them as it arises.

1. They are always in a state of flux so far as applying them is concerned.

2. Each one is subject to debate, pro and con, due to the time element and specific conditions.

3. The statement of them is poor and inadequate, so everyone will have a possible doubt and be able to think of an exception.

4. They are like iron, and woe unto the individual or nation that violates them.

Here they are:

1. Bad money drives good money out of circulation. This is called Gresham's Law. If a country has two kinds of money, one more acceptable to the public than the other, such as paper and gold, without one representing the other, the people will automatically hoard gold and exchange the paper.

2. The wealth of a nation depends mainly upon its rate of production and the rapidity with which it can dispose of its products. During a period of fright (hard times), the rapidity of disposal of the products reaches a low point, and a general wealth is therefore lowered in volume.

3. Credit has no value and does not constitute wealth unless it is profitably used. The U.S. financial system, public and private, manufactures billions of credit units which are of no value unless the people are able to use them successfully.

4. Banks should invest in credit for short periods and have a rapid turnover—velocity of use. If the credit is employed in long-term home purchases, for instance, the funds of the bank will be frozen, since depositors are privileged to withdraw their

own funds when they desire, or on very short notice.

5. Our credit system finances production in anticipation of demand. If our credit system expands, as it has since 1980, and exceeds future demand, as it has by being far in excess of our production of goods and services, *it must and will be readjusted, and nothing within the ability of mankind will prevent such readjustment.*

6. Foreign trade: Goods and services can only be paid for by other goods and services, so a country that imports more than it exports (as the U.S. is currently doing), must have recourse to credit. If this condition prevails too long, the importing country (the U.S.) will be ruined economically unless it has previously scattered abroad many assets deployed there which it can use.

7. The sale price of an article is automatically determined by supply and demand, and no state can fix its amount. If prices are fixed, bootlegging will result. There is *no period* known in all of economic history where attempting to stem supply and demand prices has ever been successful. And yet the U.S. government uses up billions of taxpayers' money trying to fix farm prices.

8. Deflation of credit extended too far ultimately destroys the whole equilibrium of

economic structure, the same as inflation does. When prices fall, real wages will buy more, but this is impossible for the worker to understand since he perceives only the fall in wage rates. In addition, price falls are never uniform. Ultimately they settle at a low level, but this takes time.

CHAPTER 12

THE END
OF THE DEBT ERA

The Crash of 1929

As we look back from the brink of Great Depression II, it is apparent that 1929 was the previous watershed year of the twentieth century. The start of that depression swept away all that had gone before, changing our economy from one based on equity to one based on debt.

To understand what lies ahead, it is first necessary to understand what has happened before: why the seemingly boundless prosperity of the late 1920s ended so abruptly, and why the Great Depression produced so many profound changes.

It began, of course, with the crash—Black Thursday, October 1929—when the stock market collapsed in the worst break in history. In dollar terms, the 1973–74 bear market cost investors more money. But in percentage terms, and in psychological terms, the 1929 collapse was far worse. By 1932 the index of stock prices had fallen to 40 from its 1929 high of 385. Commodity prices had dropped by 40%. Industrial production had shrunk 50%. International trade had slipped 30%. The International Labor Organization estimated that 30 million people in the world were unemployed.

There was no one cause for the Great Depression. Rather, it was a combination of causes and aggregates. We had a grievous miscalculation by the U.S. monetary authorities, who eased credit instead of tightening it in 1927. That was the final trigger for the credit bubble that burst in 1929.

Political unrest in Europe sapped confidence as Nazism became a major political force in Germany. Capital shortages in Central Europe, left over from World War I, had dislocated the channels of investment. The cumulative effect reduced the ability of the world economic system to absorb shocks and adjust to changes.

Also, technical improvements in agriculture produced sharply higher yields, which lowered prices for farmers while everything they bought was rising in cost. Finally, there was a proliferation of giant frauds in business, and a change of attitude leading to heavy borrowing by individuals, corporations and governments.

Economic policies and the imposition of trade barriers had propped up weak businesses instead of allowing them to fall.

Recapping the Great Depression scenario: a boom early in 1929, panic and crash in October, financial crisis in 1931, crushing deflation by 1932.

In attempts to reverse the depression, governments had to intervene actively in economic affairs, which led to new concepts of taxation, regulation, and social welfare.

Approaching Great Depression II

Before 1970 the U.S. had been a fairly structured, orderly and relatively stable society. After 1970 power blocks became prominent, each with a narrow focus on its own interest. The public reaction was populist in character, manifested by suspicion and hostility toward the growing power of big business and government. Egalitarian movements revived.

During the 1970s the U.S. economy lost much of its dynamism. Competition increased in world markets. National economic policy was unable to cope with steep declines in industrial worker productivity, with raging inflation, now with runaway deficits in the balance of payments. We sensed a clear loss of power in world politics.

Government debt, a significant source of our present woe, grew about 4-1/2 times in the post-1945 period. But private debt, which is generally ignored, was growing more than 17 fold, nearly 4 times more rapidly than public debt.

Private debt was encouraged by an unprecedented growth in the variety and size of financial institutions and markets. This burgeoning financial sector, in turn, stimulated an explosion in financial trading and speculation.

To repeat, the idea of the relative place of the financial sector in the total economy can be

gained from striking facts pointed out by Guy
E. Noyes. At the end of 1980 the annual rate of
debts from customers' demand-deposit accounts
at banks was about $68 billion, while GNP was
running at a rate of $2.2 trillion. Thus, some
4% of the work being done by money was related to transactions in the goods and services
that make up the GNP.

As Noyes explained, "A large volume of transactions, not counted in the 4% figure, involves
intermediary purchase of goods and services,
as opposed to final purchases, which is what
GNP measures. However, financial payments represent far and away the great bulk of total debits to demand deposits."[1]

The implication is clear: most of the credit in
the economy circulated in the financial sector.

That is what cannot help but bring us down:
the bursting of an overfilled credit bubble con-
taining $11 trillion in debt. And that, in turn,
can only give way to a chain-reaction financial
collapse and panic, one which must be worldwide.

Business Week, in 1974 and again in 1978,
devoted two entire issues to "The Debt Economy" and "The New Debt Economy." In the latter article, its authors commented, "For every
$3 owed in 1974, the U.S. now owes $4, a
growth in debt far faster than the growth of the
U.S. economy, even when inflation is counted
in economic growth.

"What is worrisome is that the biggest borrowers are now consumers, $1.3 trillion, whose
ability to repay has been stretched razor-thin
with the decline in real income since 1979."[2]

Real average spendable earnings of U.S. workers in 1982 were 15% lower than in 1971.

Business Week also presented a lengthy article in August 1979, in which they said the age of equity stock ownership was over for the following reasons, "Individuals are fleeing the market, younger investors lead this flight, equities are less important to most people, institutions are shifting from stocks to bonds, and corporations rely more on debt financing."[3]

Between 1945 and 1979 American finance changed one hundred and eighty degrees. We went from finance by equity to finance by debt.

That is where we were before the collapse. Corporations were using over 60% of their after-tax profits to pay interest on their enormous debts. Virtually all new lending was to roll over one high-interest short-term bank loan into another high-interest long-term loan.

Sidney Homer wrote an important book entitled *A History of Interest Rates*, in which he announced the discovery that the average rate of interest over two thousand years of human history was 3.5%.

That is what some call "the rhythm of the system," since it also represents mankind's ability to produce, compounded, over long time spans. At 6%+, interest became known as "usury" because the lender was "using" the borrower, whose loan-repaying ability from increased production was still 3.5%.

Most people, including economists and congressmen, do not know enough about banking to understand our monetary system. For example, it is still widely believed that the government prints money to cover its deficits, whereas it actually borrows money. It is also believed that the Fed helps or hurts the borrowing process through its intervention in the money markets, and by providing reserves to the banking system through its open-market operation.

The fact is that the credit America grew on came from borrowing. It was the vast pool of borrowed new credits that kept us going. What the Fed did was make certain that reserves were always there, no matter how furiously Americans ran up debt.

INTEREST BURDEN

Private-sector repayment problems emerged, and new borrowing abroad slowed in 1981. The decline of new borrowing created a shortage in the supply of credit. As the supply of credit money shrank, interest rates climbed to an average of 18%. This becomes a self-feeding spiral: huge rates discourage borrowing, which shrinks borrowing, which shrinks the credit pool, which creates even higher rates. A related spiral sets in when the consumer stops borrowing, so he can't buy as much, which raises retail inventories, which reduces the production of goods, which causes layoffs, which discourages borrowing.

By 1982 those cycles operated enough that business activity was sinking rapidly. We were past the point of reflation (pumping in more credit, hoping it will be used). There could be no business revival because the economy was literally borrowed out. Or so we thought until, in 1984, consumer installment debt grew 20.5% in one year. Mortgage debt grew similarly, then the shrinkage resumed.

This shrinking credit pool phenomena was noted by Citibank's economists in 1981, and by myself and a few others, but in most cases the concept was lost—and even today, remains lost. Why have the establishment economists missed all of this?

Didn't they even see the explosion in debt by the private sector, at rates far in excess of federal debt creation? Didn't they remember that Bretton Woods made dollars the world currency? Didn't they correctly see both as two engines of inflation?

Why did they blindly play games when it was only a matter of time before controls no longer worked and the hyper-inflated economy came crashing down?

So here we are at another major economic watershed, which could not be averted until we have another financial panic, another liquidation of debt. Debt, remember, is always repaid by either the debtor or the creditor.

The present huge debt must be liquidated, or else the U.S. economy will never recover. And we cannot solve the problem by throwing more credit at it. That's the balloon which has us on the brink of Great Depression II, ending the Era of Debt.

It's an episodic event that's bound to catch those of conventional wisdom by surprise. As in 1929, they will cry again and again, "Why? Why? How did it happen?"

Tomorrow

So the end of the 1980s will end an age just as 1929 did. By the year 2029 people will have recognized that this may have marked the end of giant industrial society as we have known it. The bigger-than-life enterprises which built the world's economy to today's levels peaked a few years ago, around 1980—82. This industrial society will be replaced by one in which diversity, not uniformity, will preserve civilization on its way to a new culture. As our present industrial society takes on a new shape, so will mass production, mass marketing and mass media.

Industrial society was based on fossil fuels, electro-mechanical technology, mass transportation, the corporation, the mass media and, above all, the marketplace. Most of these hallmarks will be gone by 2029.

New production industries will appear. The U.S. already was losing steel, automobile, railroad equipment, machinery, appliance, textile, shoe and apparel industries to producers in other countries. Being unable to compete with these foreigners, U.S. industries began liquidating themselves. But they will return, reshaped, as they did in Europe after the 1920s loss of smokestack industries there.

We will not become a nation in which we take in each other's laundry. Five new industries will grow in the new age: semiconductors and electronics, information-processing, oceanography, industrial applications of space and molecular biology. As mass production wanes and information-processing technology is widely introduced, the labor-intensive factory as we know it will disappear. Already assembly line robots are doing much of the dangerous and routine production work.

Since production is where all wealth originates, the smokestack production base will return transformed. This base supports services and, perhaps more importantly, our corporations must get rid of their debts so their pricing will again become competitive. Remember, interest costs are buried in prices and raise them.

CHAPTER 13

PAST PANICS

The Panic of 1857

Long ago, when gold was still included in our supply of money and credit, a generous new source was discovered in California. The mere fact of this discovery triggered a new speculative boom in railroading, real estate and other familiar speculator games. To jump onto this gravy train, Wall Street parlayed this new gold into credit. As usual, it was not just credit but feverish, runaway credit. The banks cooperated by permitting well-known customers to overdraw their accounts by very large amounts.

As with all speculations, frantic greed ballooned prices in many commodities, and wild, new ventures with risks at 1,000% easily sold out. It was a mindless game seemingly without end. Railroad speculations before the turn of the century demonstrate how entrenched financial gambling is in our system.

This burgeoning credit expansion, like the one we have now in the mid-1980s, finally led cooler heads to doubt, lose confidence, then to fear for their shirts. Suddenly the stock market declined sharply, bankers called in their loans and panic spread to most major cities. It seemed that everyone simultaneously wanted to liquidate whatever assets they could salvage.

Meanwhile, the gold mined in California totaled about $600 million, and everyone wanted a piece of that action. Firms were falling domino-fashion, as in all our past credit binges, and runs on banks had begun. Along with all this, was a paper-money inflation. This inflation was unique, since it occurred when paper was issued far in excess of any gold backing. Billions of dollars were thus created, and soon it was not redeemable in gold, as is always the case in such panics. Fraud, deceit and moral collapse became the tools of greed.

Quite a similar mess was taking shape during the 1980s at Bank of America, which was first swindled in a fraudulent real estate scheme. It cost the bank $135 million in mortgage defaults in the early 1980s. Commenting on the case, the *New York Times* observed that it was only the tip of real estate fraud nationwide. It was a simple scheme, merely convincing the banks to lend far in excess of property values. Such loans were no good before the ink dried.

Then as now, the lesson is the same: rampant speculation using credit spurs greed, the credit balloons to unmanageable proportions, the balloon is pricked by some triggering event, and down comes the entire thing in a panic of liquidations, frauds and deceits.

The Panic of 1861

Most businessmen lose money at the start of a war and this was so as the Civil War got underway. But this time there was an unusual twist. Cotton growers in the newly formed Confederacy owed Northern banks $300 million. Besides losing that money, Northern banks took an additional beating when, in 1861 alone, six thousand businesses failed.

Northern banks suspended Special Payments in December of that year, and the government in Washington, D.C., soon followed suit. To finance the war, both Confederate and federal governments issued paper money. Ultimately, the federals issued some $450 million in greenback notes which bore no interest, and sold over $1 billion in bonds through the business genius of Jay Cooke.

After the war the federal treasury began to redeem greenbacks and replace them with other credit instruments, but the farmers, always easy-money advocates, halted that.

In the South there was nothing to argue over. At least $4 billion disappeared forever into the lost cause. Some die-hard rebels, believing the South would rise again, held onto their Confederate bills. Credit panics are not lost wars, but they might as well be. Both the Old Confederacy and what they had called money went up in smoke.

The Panic of 1873

Wars always breed large readjustment tensions into economic systems. World Wars I and II were followed by periods of imbalance, and so was the Civil War.

In 1873, eight years after the War Between the States, the financial landscape was dominated by some new, war-rich millionaires, who had become railroad builders and were called the Robber Barons. It is difficult for people today to appreciate the swashbuckling tactics of those Robber Barons. Today, their kind keep a low profile, but through the 1860s and 1870s, their schemes to raise money, scuttle rivals and buy political influence seem, in retrospect, unbelievable.

Inflation had continued unchecked after the Civil War as debtors insisted that the Treasury at least keep the greenbacks in circulation. The debtors hoped this fiat money would be increased so they could repay their loans in cheaper currency.

With cheap credit, then like now, everything got overbuilt, overbought and overhyped, spurred by heady speculation. Stock, commodity and land prices soared . . . until farm products began a quiet slide.

By 1872 there was a money pinch in which some rates shot up to 160%. The triggering event of the Panic of 1873 came when Jay Cooke, backing the construction of the Northern Pacific Railroad, failed to meet a $1 million note due on September 18. His office closed at 11

A.M. A major Washington bank then also closed, followed by the first-ever halt in trading on the New York Stock Exchange. The depression which followed lasted five years.

The dynamics of events leading to the Panic of 1873 bear an astonishing similarity to those of our present period.

In a nutshell, when production of real wealth cannot repay debts in paper wealth, or even pay the interest, the result is always the same—financial collapse.

The Panic of 1884

In 1884 a whiz kid financier named Ferdinand Ward gained the confidence and support of General Ulysses S. Grant. Like most money manipulators, Ward built a pyramid on shaky credit. When his collapsed, it took down with it many brokerage firms, banks and other businesses. During this panic, failure followed failure until J. P. Morgan saved the day, preventing this one from becoming a depression.

The moral of this tale is fairly simple: Excess bank credit leads to money manipulation, land and commodity speculation, corporate failures and ultimately financial collapse. Beyond prudent limits, credit expansion stresses the economic system. At worst, when speculations don't succeed, they may lose enough to leave the entire financial system short of credit money. This, in turn, triggers a leap in interest rates, borrowing ceases and the whole system caves in. The repetition of this scenario in U.S. history is astonishing.

The Rich Man's Panic of 1907

The year 1907 began with a nagging apprehension in the financial markets that all was not well. Then this uncertainty was given specific shape by the failure of Consolidated Copper Company. Already in control of over half the copper production in the U.S., Consolidated had tried to corner the entire market. It went into hock for this purpose, and the credit it created was lost. Again the banks were left with a loss big enough to fuel a general panic.

But this one was confined to people of means, hence the label, Rich Man's Panic. Interest rates soared, then fell precipitously. There were bank reserve problems, gold transfers, abuse of bank credit, stock speculation and land speculation— all the old familiar characters in the panic drama, and at the root of it all, the overfilled balloon of bank credit.

Why does this abuse of bank credit keep repeating? In our system bankers have a license to create purchasing power by making loans. However, it is the nature of banks, given the profit motive, to get carried away and write too many loans, creating an excess of demand deposits which can never be redeemed in cash. With a ratio of deposits to cash of ten to one, any one of many triggering events can bring on panic.

Are there ways to control a fractional-deposit credit machine? Two schemes have been suggested: (1) ration credit at the federal level, and (2) ration retail credit at the local level, where the banker knows his customers.

Will either be implemented? Not likely. In today's lonely crowd society, how many bankers know their customers? Besides, the banking fraternity in the U.S. has a long history of going its own way—by strength, subterfuge or a combination of both.

The Crash of 1929

Many alive today have vivid memories, from their teens or early childhood, of the Great Depression's years of privation and pain. Few were old enough to appreciate its causes, however.

From the middle of 1922 to early 1928, $14.5 billion in loans and investments were created, plus $13.5 billion in bank deposits. This was a truly colossal growth in runaway bank credit. It was, at that time, the greatest expansion of bank credit in history.

That from 1917 to the end of 1918 to fight World War I was only $5.8 billion in deposits, plus $7 billion in loans.

Norman S. Buch, in *Survey of Contemporary Economics*, gave an assessment of the situation in the 1920s, which could be mistaken for one describing the 1980s, when he wrote:

"The vastly greater expansion from 1922 to 1928 was needed by commerce and was not used by commerce, and went into (1) real estate mortgage loans in banks; (2) investment-finance paper in banks; (3) stock and bond collateral loans in banks, including loans against foreign stocks and bonds; and (4) bond purchases by banks, including many foreign bond issues. The result was excess construction, real estate speculation on a great scale, overexpansion of installment buying, over-issue and sale of securities, rapid multiplication of bonds, houses, investment trusts, etc."[1]

This shift from production of goods and services to production of financial flim-flam . . . doesn't it sound familiar?

CHAPTER 14

THE STOCK MARKET CRASH OF 1987

What made the crash of the stock market on October 19, 1987, so extraordinary was that never before in U.S. stock market history had nearly one-third of equity values been wiped out in a matter of two days. Nearly $1 trillion was lost. The credit fallout would continue and grow.

Not only that, but, uniquely, the losses were just as devastating in the global economy, where the global stock market crashed over 35% from an estimated $12 trillion in stock and bond values in the global economy before the crash—a $4 trillion loss. This wild behavior of the stock markets and the gap between them and real economic activity cannot be understood in conventional economic theories, so our experts were helpless to explain this disaster.

What was additionally unusual about the Crash of 1987 was the uncanny optimism that followed it. For example, in an article by Leonard Silk, *New York Times* in-house economic expert, he wrote, "Lawrence Veit of Brown Brothers, Harriman & Company said, 'It should be remembered that the U.S. economy had actually turned down prior to the 1929 and 1987 stock market panics. Thus with the economy still in an expansionary mode, 1987 looks less like 1929 or 1937—more like the panic of 1962 which was followed by five years of prosperity.' "[1]

Economist John Galbraith wrote a long time ago, "Cause and effect run from the economy to the stock market, never the reverse." The evidence is that this is true since the U.S. economy, as noted earlier, has been stagnating for years. It seems to make common sense that if the U.S. economy truly had sound underpinnings, stock market plunge of that scale and speed would never have happened. Instead, the crash sent a clear message of extreme financial and economic vulnerability, which is the central theme of this book. We are on the brink of another Great Depression.

Everyone seems to have forgotten George Santayana's warning, "Those who cannot remember the past are condemned to repeat it." A new young generation of experts got trapped as their predecessors in stock market history had again and again.

The Stock Speculative Bubble

The stock market was elevated to the sky by the extraordinary expansion of credit created by the private sector, as I have described. Economists call this reality excess liquidity, a slick name for too much debt. But since the U.S. manufacturing sector was stagnating, the extra credit creation flowed like a raging torrent into the U.S. financial services industry. The stock market trapped a lot of this flow of credit, and went skyward. Somewhere in this climb the dynamics of speculation reappeared: too much borrowing coupled with the leverage that it carried along.

The heart of speculation in U.S. stock and commodity markets is always leverage, the use of credit money to magnify many times its purchasing power. You can speculate on a cash basis, but the rewards are tiny compared to those gained by leverage. For example, if you buy something for cash and it goes up 30%, you have made, in theory, a 30% profit on your invested funds. But if you buy the same thing on a 10% margin (10% down payment) and it goes up 30%, you have made a gain of 300% on your actual invested capital. This is still another reason the Crash of 1987 was on such a gigantic scale. The public also forgot that the leverage that created the 300% gain also works in reverse, because it also has the downside potential of a 300% drop which needs cash to support it, not credit.

In addition to normal leverage, merger mania also created billions of dollars to buy stocks and thus inflate their prices to ridiculous heights. In 1984 corporate purchases of stocks were $90 billion; in 1986, $125 billion, and by October 1987 it had reached, in nine months, $160 billion, nearly double the 1984 total.

While all of this was going on, the individual investor had been selling stocks for years. Even if you add up his purchases of mutual funds, he had sold roughly $250 billion in stocks since 1984, just about the amount that corporations and foreign investors were buying in that time period.

Phase II: The Worst Is Still to Come

The stock market Crash of 1987 was Phase I. There were no bank runs, no real estate collapse, no installment-credit collapse, like credit card defaults en masse. Everyone seemed calm by the late fall of 1987. The stock market remained shaky, but disturbing signs of more and larger trouble were in the making.

In this book I have emphasized bank and private-sector credit creation, which gives business growth and expansion, and its reverse, credit contraction, which brings stagnation and hard times to us all.

The central problem in describing the process of credit contraction is that it is a process which at its start is virtually invisible. For example, raw material prices started falling worldwide in 1974. But in the late 1970s U.S. farmers were still borrowing furiously as U.S. farm land and food prices rose. Then the world price decline stretched out and hit U.S. markets and farm crop prices started down, taking farm land along with them. Then big trouble started as farmers and their banks failed silently and surely. By 1985 the problem reached Washington, D.C., in the form of $212 billion in farm debts that were certain to go unpaid. In fact, by late 1987 these debts had virtually consumed the Federal

Farm Credit System. Farm credit death struck years ago, but no one was looking because we were all busy trying to cope with inflation which was being replaced by deflation. But even in late 1987 many experts still feared the return of inflation (rising import prices, we were told, would cause this event). Old ideas and memories die hard.

WHY I CALL THIS "PHASE II"

Following the farm debt crisis, we have yet to see these other losses unfold, which will erupt in 1988 and 1989:

1. Latin loans: about $350 billion will never be repaid. Since no Latin nation has paid a loan since 1800, why should we think they will now?

2. Junk bond defaults: over $150 billion

3. Municipal debts: over $1 trillion

4. FDIC and FSLIC liabilities: over $2 trillion

5. Corporate bond debt defaults: about $500 billion

6. Consumer installment credit defaults: over $600 billion

In 1989 and 1990 we will see many of these debts going into default, not all of them but enough to cause an episodic financial crisis.

This is because debts are always paid by either the debtor or the creditor. There will be no walking away, no printing of paper money, no inflating our way out of this. The debt liquidation ahead will, as it always has in the past, plunge us into a long depression. A time when we will all scrape the bottom of the barrel and wonder where our next dime is coming from.

We have lived frivolously and off the cuff since 1945. We have lived beyond our means, and our dream machine will go into reverse as we start paying our bills. We will pay the financial piper. The overborrowing and overspending will halt. But never in all of recorded economic history have debts on this enormous scale gone bad, so the fallout will be devastating.

HIGH-TECH MONEY

The Japanese call electronic money *zaitech*, literally "high-tech finance." We call the new credit money "computer money," that is, the kind of money you are familiar with when you go into your bank and ask for your balance and they must find it on a computer. Our currency has shifted from paper to computer credit money. The public, since they deal a lot with cash, thinks in terms of paper money as the real money. It isn't, as I have described. It is credit which we use as a substitute for money because it, too, has purchasing power.

The shift from paper and checkbook money to computer money is, I believe, the most significant technological change of our time, and that includes our space ventures and our missiles, and so on. Almost unnoticed, this change has changed our lives forever.

The dollar value of all international trade in 1986 was $2 trillion. The dollar value of all international capital transfers in 1986 was $30 trillion! And many people are still wandering around talking about coming paper money hyper-inflation!

Without computer credit money there would be no credit cards, for starters. There would be no easy credit. For instance, it is calculated that now a credit check can be run on anyone in eleven seconds so credit is easy to get. It has changed the way we think about money and credit. You can buy a car, say, for $16,000, and sign a raft of papers; no cash, no checks change hands. You drive away in a $16,000 car, like magic. It isn't until a month or so later you get the payment book and realize you have put yourself deeper in the debt trap. I call it a trap since compound interest means your car will cost and cost and cost before you finish paying for it—if you ever do.

We have almost begun to think that money is free. We don't dig down in our pockets for cash to pay for something, or write a check. Instead, we hand over a credit card or sign a form and there's the purchase! We don't worry about this since it is normal behavior in the U.S. to be optimistic, so we are certain our future income increases will pay our debts. We have mortgaged our income to the moon, but we don't worry. Everything will be all right!

On a larger scale, the same change has happened with big-time money, and the process

216 Howto Profit from the Next Great Depression

works the same way. The only difference is that the numbers are larger; millions, billions, trillions. With electronic credit, corporate merger credit was easy, junk bonds were easy and one new credit dynamo after another sprung to life in the halcyon days of 1986 and 1987. The Federal Reserve itself wire-transferred almost $1 trillion per day! In New York City, bank clearings reached $1 trillion a day (this represented checks cleared the computer way, of course).

This speed brought with it diversity and great complexity in credit forms. The financial game became so complex that no one person could fathom it, and the *speed*, world around, meant heavy new consequences. New instabilities arose out of the unevenness in the transactional speeds in different parts of the system. By forcing the speed and acceleration of financial transactions, we restructured the financial system itself. Money no longer waited. It was on real time, speed-of-light time. We abused this gift and it brought us stress and also the financial deregulation that, in turn, brought us the debts we now cannot repay. Alas.

One of the other weaknesses in mainstream economic analysis was that the economic models and ideas created were constructed mainly around U.S. problems. They overlooked the dramatic growth in the global economy that computer-credit money fostered. Thus, an idea arose to tax the rich to balance the federal budget, but this ignored the computer ease of capital flight, not to mention the subsequent loss of tax revenues. Of course, as leverage grew in global credit transfers, this compounded the growth of the world credit bubble.

THE NEW ERA

My impression is that the new financial technology has launched us into an entirely new era. It is one where old economic theories no longer work. Alvin Toffler wrote about this societal change in *The Third Wave*. This is where we are now. We are in a transition from the industrial era to a new, nameless era which is also formless and very different. Most economic theories today, the notions of mainstream experts, were developed during the past industrial age. For example, late in 1987 economists were warning us that a falling U.S. dollar meant U.S. imports would cost more and thus bring us another bout of inflation. Not only that, it was the only medicine to increase our exports and revive manufacturing industries.

But we found instead that after two years of a falling price for the dollar in foreign exchange markets, the trade deficits remained large and import prices did *not* cause more inflation. In sum, the entire accepted economic wisdom was flawed. And almost any accepted textbook idea now is hard to fit into the world as we know it. Economic theory and economic reality were never partners, but it is a far worse fit now.

What mystified Wall Street experts, it seems, about the Crash of 1987 was their failure to understand the true nature of bank credit money and private-credit monies. Both of these forms of credit were equal only to the value of the collateral behind the credit. So, if the market value of stock collateral supported a credit extension, then when stock prices fell, so did the value of the collateral, intensifying the debt-repayment problem of the borrower. Wall Street's losses were not paper losses by any means. The credits that vanished when stock prices fell represented purchasing power lost forever, as many soon discovered.

In sum, the Crash of 1987 added *a new credit contraction* to the economy in general, which was already feeling other credits contract, as I have written. The combination formed a credit squeeze that will silently plunge us into a massive, deflationary depression. *These forces are irreversible.*

So the Crash of 1987, Phase I, has set the stage for Phase II. That tidal wave is on the horizon, coming down on us, and we will soon find ourselves deep in another Great Depression. And we will be unable to dig ourselves out of this deep hole for years. It will bring in its wake, a new economic, social and political system. Everything that now seems to be so set in cement will change. And change is an *ordeal*, not something easy.

Obviously, you must get ready now. Get prepared materially and psychologically. Be one day early instead of one day late. Ideas on saving your finances—even realizing a profit—are outlined in Chapter 16.

CHAPTER 15

STAGNATION, REFLATION, COMPOUND INTEREST

In the 1980s we unwittingly became involved in a lifestyle of electronics, and this changed the way we looked at things. We expected practically everything to be complete and made available "yesterday."

In economic affairs, one crisis after another erupted: trade imbalances, seesawing exchange rates with the dollar rising and falling drastically, record federal deficits—to cite the most obvious. But all these events were short-run when put into historic perspective.

It became common for our leading economic experts to forecast what our rate of growth (GNP) would be for the next quarter, even for the next four quarters. Seen from the electronic lifestyle, that seemed like a long time ahead. But in historic reality, what has happened is that we've all become enveloped in a fantasy world of short-term expectations. Concurrently we came to believe that our economic affairs were controllable, our money problems solvable. We believed the government won't let another depression happen. We believed that, had we put into place safety nets in the 1930s, they would have thwarted the savage economic downturn.

All the while we ignored the fact that depressions have happened with great regularity all through the history of capitalism. We forgot that we had a Federal Reserve back in 1929, and that it couldn't stop that depression. No one back then (or now) discovered a solution to the problem of how to prevent prices from falling. Sure, economists knew then, and now, all about rising prices and expanding growth. So did the public. We all had to become inflation experts. But falling prices are as great a mystery now as then.

The Stuff of History

The old saying has it that we repeat history because we failed to learn from it. We forget our mistakes. That's true, but it's also true that the history of depressions cover long-range periods, even generational gaps. From this secular trend, and considering the major events that impact our lives, short-range events in money and economics are trivial.

What really matters to us all in the end are the centuries-old secular trends. And they are imperceptible to our contemporaries—our present generation of economists and politicians—who only have eyes for the surface events of our electronic lifestyle.

But it would be a good idea to become fascinated with the cyclical rhythms which have accompanied, or constituted, the history of capitalism. For these long waves, the cycles of prices over half a century are the stuff of history . . . which we either learn or are doomed to repeat.

Fernand Braudel described these rhythms as "the economic fluctuations of varying length which seem to succeed one another like waves rolling in from the sea . . . a rule of world history, a rule which has reached down the ages to us and will carry on."[1]

Years ago he speculated about whether or not we would see another downward slope of the Kondratieff cycle between 1972 and 1974. (We did.) If so, he stated, "Are not the day-to-day remedies proposed to meet the crisis completely illusory?"

Those failures are familiar: Prominent men in high positions acting as though they control economic and financial events, and not realizing they are controlled by these events.

It is this grand scope of economic history which sets the stage for our economic lives. After all, since 1776 the two major events which have most impacted the psyche of the average American were the Civil War and the Great Depression. And now we are lunging toward another such major secular event, another depression which will leave us helpless.

Or at least it will seem that way to policymakers. It could be that the very nature of the system precludes solution, and thus arranges for watershed change, promising a quite different tomorrow. If the ebb and flow of history tells us one thing, it is this: we are now on the cutting edge of a major, episodic change of all that presently seems familiar.

Historical Reasons
That Make a Depression Inevitable

Every great depression in the age of industrial capitalism has come near the end of a period of relative economic stagnation in the domestic and world economies. This was true of the great depressions of the 1930s, the 1890s and the 1830s. Periods of relative stagnation followed periods of very strong and sustained economic growth during which the conditions that brought on stagnation developed.

For example, the U.S. and the Western world experienced rapid economic growth from 1945 to 1970. In the early 1970s real wages peaked in the U.S., and in 1974 raw material prices peaked in the world. Stagnation set in. Despite what seems to be recovery since 1974, the real economy has been stagnating. For one hundred years before 1970, the average growth of U.S. GNP had been 3.5% per year. From 1970 to 1986, U.S. GNP averaged 2.3% per year, a substantial decline, and this decline was due to stagnation.

The ongoing stagnation was hidden by the credit explosion the world over, and in 1982 a U.S. stock market rise started which continued until recently.

Why has the economy shifted from high growth to low growth and stagnation?

The chief function of a depression is to liquidate the imbalances which the preceding growth period put into place. Specifically, depressions bring business and personal bankruptcies, which eliminate the excessive debt burdens and credit expansion generated by the previous era of long-continued prosperity.

Depressions cause massive unemployment. This brings wages down and offers the prospect of low wages for the relatively near future. Depressions always bring in their wake sharply falling commodity prices. (In the U.S. wholesale prices fell 2.6% in 1986, the first decline since 1949.) Raw material prices also fall and this means, among other things, that you'll be able to build a new home cheaper than you can buy an existing home. Depressions greatly reduce interest rates, far below the levels we are now told are low.

Stagnation in U.S. capitalistic society is brought on by sustained rapid economic growth, which also brings us high levels of debt, high wages ($17.50 an hour for postmen, for example), high commodity prices (e.g., $34 per barrel for oil) and high interest rates, as in 1981.

Great depressions stand these relationships on their heads. By doing so, hard times bring a depression psychosis, a prolonged period of disenchantment by the public with things as they are.

This disenchantment, in turn, brings social and political change, and the winds of change are already blowing. Depressions set the stage for more growth, if the system can stand the crisis. It did in the 1930s, just barely. But I, for one, have serious doubts about the system weathering the coming financial crisis.

Never in all of recorded economic history

have debt loads the size of ours ever under-gone liquidation. The 1930s debts were a piece of cake compared with our current load at every level. So we are truly entering something unprecedented.

The public is already running scared. The so-called American dream home has vanished for most newlyweds. Two-family incomes often can't afford a dinner out at McDonald's and future income growth seems elusive or no longer obtainable. The public in 1988 is under terrible economic stress. Do you sense this yourself?

Our present long-wave expansion began with the start of World War II. The chief stimulus then as now was spending for arms. Following the war, from 1946 to 1970, the U.S. went through the longest and most rapid growth of economic expansion in its history. And this was true of the world economy as well.

This great period of economic growth had characteristics similar to the expansion phases of the previous long waves in economic history, although the details were different. For example:

1. A group of leading industries, or sectors, all expanding together and reinforcing each other, promoting further growth in related industries: consumer-goods industries like housing (suburbia), automobiles, home appliances, etc.; industries involving new technology like electronics, computers and jet propulsion; and government services such as education and health care.

2. Credit expansion exploded in all sectors on a gigantic scale, leading to our present $11 trillion in domestic debts.

3. Large military expenditures: World War II, Korea, the Cold War, Vietnam and the $1 trillion spent by Reaganauts since 1980 to foster protection. And in the wake of that, forced economic growth, with military spending shifting more to nuclear missiles and electronics.

4. A large-scale expansion of world trade aided by foreign lending on an unprecedented scale, leading us to the uncollectable loans we now face.

Underlying these trends were a series of favorable basic economic relationships: supplies of energy were plentiful and prices were low. The same was true of food supplies. In the advanced industrial countries labor was relatively scarce, with population growth exceeding the growth of the labor force for some fifteen years after the end of World War II.

As a result, wage rates tended to rise, stimulating both the purchasing power of workers and the substitution of capital for labor in the production process. This substitution raised productivity and profits enough to make the rising wage rates possible without significant inflation. The cost of capital was low, as long as the rates of the 1930s (1%) continued. All these economic relationships favored growth: low costs of capital, energy, food and favorable supply-

and-demand relationships in the labor market that stimulated both consumer demand and business development.

And now, in just a few short years, those relationships have turned unfavorable. One leading sector after another reached production capacities capable of meeting the existing demand, and reduced spending for investment. The U.S. has not produced at 100% capacity now for sixteen years.

Then other fundamentals changed. The price of oil soared. So did food prices in the 1970s. Labor costs got out of hand and interest rates headed for the sky. These conditions began to appear from about 1966 to 1972. And the expansion ended. Stagnation set in.

Since then—although I know it's hard to believe because it's masked or hidden by credit expansion—our decline has progressed. The slowdown has been almost invisible. The illusion of prosperity and good times is just that. Unnoticed, our way of life has been changing. The final dramatic shift will soon erupt. Depression psychosis will reappear, and we will enter a major era of uncontrollable decline.

Right now it's impossible to guess how far we'll fall, but it will be well below the lows of the 1930s, which will come as a surprise to most people, even—or perhaps I should say especially—to most economic experts.

Die-Hard Myths

Since the Great Depression, a number of myths about the economy have arisen, some of them so firmly entrenched that they're put forth in economic textbooks. Two of the most die-hard myths are the following:

1. Rising prices are always caused by inflation, and

2. The federal government has the power to control the economy.

Subsidiary to both those myths is another: the federal government now has in place safety nets in the form of unemployment insurance, welfare, food stamps, social security, etc. If the economy gets too rocky, these safety nets will kick in and prevent complete disaster.

Likewise, it is believed by most economists and policymakers that the government will never permit another deflationary depression, as occurred during the 1930s. Which brings us back to the notion that rising prices are always caused by inflation and, therefore, the federal government can prevent deflation by reflation.

In the February 1987 issue of *Playboy* magazine, a Ph.D. economist named Paul Erdman followed up on his hit novel, *The Panic of '89*, with an article titled "Don't Panic." Both the novel and the article correctly cite massive debt as the cause of a coming crash, and Erdman comes up with a reasonable scenario for why he expects the crash to begin in late 1989.

Erdman's logic goes haywire, however, when he comes up with his scenario about how we will get out of the crash with minimal danger, and get the economy back on track. His logic falls apart because he falls back on those two myths: rising prices are always caused by inflation and the federal government controls the economy. How does Erdman suppose we will find our way quickly out of the coming crash? By reflation. By the Fed causing a spiral of inflation to stave off a deflationary depression.

Erdman tells us that 90% of "fifty heavy hitters in banking, the oil business, government and universities" feel that "the solution will come in the form of massive reflation."

He continues, "When massive amounts of new money start to chase the same amount of goods, prices must rise. Everybody knows that."

What "everybody" seems to have forgotten, of course, is that inflation peaked in the early 1970s and the trend since then has been deflationary. But this trend has been masked by rising prices caused by the cost of credit interest and not by massive injections of new credit money. A loaf of bread costs more in the supermarket today, even though the cost of raw wheat has come way down. What has been tacked onto the price is not massive amounts of new money chasing the same amount of goods, but the cost of borrowing the money to produce and deliver that loaf of bread.

OLD MYTHS AND NEW

The reflation myth is not new. It was extant back in the 1830s. The prevailing theory then, as now, was that business could be revived by liberalizing credit. It didn't work in the 1830s, the 1890s, or in the 1930s, and its chances of succeeding in the 1990s have not improved with time.

What past depressions have taught those of us willing to learn is that it is extremely difficult or downright impossible for the Federal Reserve, the U.S. Treasury, or any other government agency to save the economy from depression by augmenting the purchasing power of the people.

The reality then, as now, is that the federal government can only aid in readjusting capital accounts of private business, but can add nothing to the expansion of business. For example, the government can lend funds to distressed farmers (as it did in the 1930s and the 1980s), enabling those farmers to pay off loans to insurance companies or the Farm Credit System. And those repaid lenders, in turn, can reinvest in government bonds. But the end result for the farmer is that he has a new creditor: the federal government. He has no new assets, merely the same old liability. In short, there has been a shift in credit, but no new credit created.

Still the myth of the federal bailout persists. So it shouldn't be too surprising that 90% of Dr. Erdman's "experts" are predicting free lunch in the form of reflation.

But the reality is that the upcoming depression will do what past depressions have done. It will sink many heavily indebted corporations, ending their ability to create jobs for workers who will, in turn, be sunk because they can't pay their bills. This rising unemployment of consumers will unravel the $2.4 trillion in installments and mortgage credit at the same time that corporations will be going into default, banks will be collapsing, foreign creditors will be clamoring for repayment, foreign investors will be yanking their money out of the U.S. economy and, according to present calculations, AIDS will be costing as much as defense currently costs.

Moreover, when foreign debtors default, as they must, large banks and small presently maintained by fictional accounting methods will be wiped out. Their depositors will lose billions of dollars, and the FDIC and FSLIC will be helpless to insure those losses.

Since 95% of what we call money is now really credit—numbers in computers—the coming collapse may very well cause a massive computer failure, as financial institutions of all kinds scramble to survive.

FREE LUNCH . . .?

Reflationary bailouts by the federal government cannot save us, as the *Playboy* article and its fifty experts believe. The Fed does not control the supply of credit money in this world economy, any more than it did back in 1930 when our economy was national. As bankruptcies contract credit, prices will fall because the cost of interest has been extracted. The federal government will have its hands full and its deficits astronomical trying to provide what safety nets it can. It won't be able to bail out private lenders by making new loans. And it certainly won't be able to inject massive amounts of new money to create new credit.

In the first place, the true engine of our economic system is expansion of credit by the private sector, not by the federal government. And in the second place, who's going to borrow when business is so bad, and who's going to lend to bankrupt companies? Where will lendable money come from when our present balloon of credit money bursts and shrinks? The reality is we will be frozen into a period of hard times—again. And this time, it could very well be worse than ever before in our history.

What really brought us out of the Great Depression was massive amounts of government spending for arms to fight World War II. This spending did not produce consumer goods, however. The goods it produced were destroyed, either by war or by time. But it did stimulate a great new expansion of credit, which carried over into our post-war production of consumer goods and the creation of credit to buy them.

But a World War III would not have the same beneficent effect, to say the least. And so we shall have to find a new way out of the coming storm.

It is widely believed by mainstream economists that the safety nets put into place in the 1930s will work again. They refer to FDIC and

FSLIC, Social Security, unemployment compensation, etc. I do not agree. Those safety nets addressed the problems of the 1930s and not the problems that we will be facing.

People will adapt to changed economic conditions, as they always have since the time of the Egyptian pyramids. And those who love to tinker will develop new ideas. Meanwhile, the government will run deficits of perhaps $400 billion to fund what safety nets it can, just when it can least afford to, and we will muddle onward into a world much different from the one we've known since the end of World War II.

What powers a credit economy such as ours? Compound interest. So let's have a look at compound interest, for in the final analysis it is at the heart of both credit expansion and credit contraction, both good times and bad.

The Absurdity of Compound Interest

A friend of mine had a charge account with J.C. Penney. He had an average balance of about $300. A few years ago he bought a VCR for about $350 and put it on the extended low pay program. He made payments of $55 a month during 1986. In January of 1987 he was notified by Penney's (as the law requires) that his interest payments alone in 1986 came to $127.56. That's an example of the absurdity of compound interest.

In a debt-ridden society, though, few pay any real attention to the effects of compound interest. Few know what is called "the rule of 72."

This is a mathematical way of saying that if you pay an interest rate of, say 9% and divide that into the number 72, the result will be how long it will take for the funds to double. In this case, in eight years $1,000 becomes $2,000.

Our economic system is built upon compound interest, which has become enshrouded—made a mystery to the consuming masses—in a cloud of credit which expands and is now deflating according to the confidence of the people. This credit cloud is dynamic, but is supposed to fit into a cooperative economic system which is static. The two do not work together.

JUST WHAT IS COMPOUND INTEREST?

Compound interest: "That which plows on Sunday."

The mathematical nature of exponential processes is easily forgotten. The most familiar example to most of us takes place in a bank—the growth of a savings deposit at compound interest. The sum of $100 deposited at 6% interest will earn $6 in the first year; in the second year, with the deposit increased to $106, it will earn $6.36, and so on. As long as the process continues, the sum grows geometrically (2, 4, 8, 16, etc.) leading to the dramatic, if usually unrealizable consequence, that after 100 years, the principal will amount to about $34,000 and earn an annual interest of $2,040.

The reason for the dramatic growth of a sum held at compound interest is that there is a repeated, cyclical interaction between the two elements of the system: the size of the deposit (the principal) and the granting of interest. A series of ongoing actions takes place: the granting of interest increases the size of the principal; the enlarged principal then increases the amount of interest granted; and so on. Mathematically, these actions represent a series of multiplications, the number of which can be expressed by an exponent. Thus 2 means that the number 2 enters into the multiplication process three times (2 x 2 x 2), which amounts to 8; here the exponent is 3. A relationship that is governed by such sequential multiplicative events is called exponential.

Following is a table which shows the mathematics of compound interest.

Future Value of $1,000 Compounded Annual Rates of Return

At End of	Annual Rates of Return				
	5%	8%	10%	12%	15%
5 Years	$1,276	$1,649	$1,610	$1,762	$2,011
10 Years	1,829	2,159	2,594	3,106	4,046
20 Years	2,653	4,661	6,727	9,646	16,366
30 Years	4,322	10,063	17,149	29,960	66,212
40 Years	7,040	21,724	45,239	93,051	267,364

The noted European banker, Baron Rothschild, called compound interest "the eighth wonder of the world," and he was right. He knew its incredible power.

Since biblical times, the idea of interest compounding has been reviled. But it's still very much with us, as we see in 20% credit card rates (the same consumer loan rate that prevailed in the Roman Empire at its peak).

The theoretical principle in connection with

our economic system is that, as a whole, the U.S. public, under our so-called free enterprise system, saves more than they spend for actual existence. These savings continue to earn more en masse, and eventually their size becomes tremendous.

Credit is bad enough in and of itself. But when compounding interest is tacked on the end product, it's unbelievable. For example, in America today there is about $11 tiillion in domestic debt. At an interest rate of 10%, the annual interest cost is $1.1 trillion—and that's just for one year.

How do we pay this interest? The cost is included in the things we buy. This is because the cost of interest is added into every step of the production process where borrowed funds were used. A farmer pays 15 cents interest on each $1 worth of food he produces.

So we (1) use credit and (2) interest cost keeps compounding. Eventually the amount reaches tremendous proportions. If there were no deflations and credit liquidations, this burden of credit would become so immense that a pound of cheese could cost $100,000.

But the credit bubble and its interest addition always bursts and puts the economy through the wringer: hard times.

PROGRESSION AND REGRESSION

If you apply the mathematical progression to the whole world, which uses the same system in the main, it is not difficult to see the complete absurdity. Since Nature—or whatever you choose to name the cause—will not approve of such an absurdity, when compound interest builds these credits too large, there is a crash. The crash destroys a large proportion of it, thus keeping the whole scheme within the bounds of practicality.

Years ago, the contrary workings of the additions of compound interest were found in the principles of amortization and sinking funds. These principles presupposed a certain time— 30, 50 or 100 years—when the credit turns into actual debt and must be paid. In the past, borrowers with high credit did not believe it necessary to establish sinking funds. They were certain they could pay off their creditors by borrowing anew from other sources. But depressions proved that this was not possible. So it was hoped that by putting aside from earnings a certain amount each year, there would be no difficulty in meeting the debt obligation when it fell due.

This principle resulted in many sad consequences. Around the turn of the century in New York City, funds were set aside from tax receipts to meet credit bills when they fell due. But the officials who guarded the funds used them instead to purchase other New York debts. And since all forms and kinds of debts of the same issuing institution usually tend to improve or deteriorate alike, the sinking fund did not truly fulfill its mission.

If we ever reach the point where a pound of cheese costs $100,000, the amortizing of $10,000 over a 10-year period would be just another bit of nonsense. While all this may seem involved, if you stop to think about it, the understanding and convincing will be self-inflicted and easy.

Uncharted Future

It is imperative, then, that we have periods for destroying credit as well as times when we create new credit. We always hope the adjustment will not be too severe, but alas. Never in all of U.S. or world history has there been an $11 trillion debt bubble ready to be partially liquidated. By comparison, the debts of 1929 were minuscule. Thus our future is unchartable.

Our financial system has definite faults, and it's right and proper to point them out. Under a noncredit system, under a nonprofit economy, under a socialist government, there would, in theory, be no compound interest and no necessity for amortizing a sinking fund. If one prefers to live in such a system to escape the repercussions of recurring hard times, there would be no criticism of this desire.

My point is that many people are willing to suffer the inconveniences of the credit system rather than endure the lack of individual freedom under a socialized form of government.

In any event, we cannot but sense the inevitability of a breakdown coming, in our time, again after fifty or sixty years. And much of it is due to, and can be traced to, compound interest.

These panics and depressions do not consider the individual any more than hurricanes at sea consider a particular ship. If one ship is built stronger than another, it has a better chance of escaping destruction. But if the hurricane becomes a holocaust—as it seems to me this time it will—all ships will go down no matter how well constructed.

It is the desire of people to control these destructive forces, but, like hurricanes, they cannot be controlled.

Absurdity en toto: it is theorized that $1 compounded at 1% every minute for 24 hours would amount to $2.17. Is this fiction? Absolutely not. Thus our total domestic debt of $8 trillion at an average interest rate of 10% per year is generating $800 billion a year, $67 billion a month, $3.3 billion per working day. That's how much we have to pay just to keep from going deeper in debt—without borrowing more. But of course much of this keep-even payback is being done with newly borrowed dollars, digging us ever deeper into the compound interest hole of debt.

That's the credit bubble we have created and which, when it bursts, will carry away in a storm of bankruptcies, defaults and uncollectable obligations, the American way of life as we have known it.

CHAPTER 16

THE
SILVER LINING

The clouds of the approaching storm are dark indeed, but there is a silver lining. For it has been true historically that what is made in good times is debt, and what is made in bad times is real wealth. Liquidating the debts accumulated in good times offers bargain-basement buys for those who are prepared. And although much has changed in our world, there is no reason to believe that modern finance will alter that historic truism.

Here in America we have insisted for generations that our financial institutions be closely regulated by government authorities. This, we deemed, would provide us with some sort of financial safety. And that system seemed to work fairly well until about fifteen years ago.

That's when a popular notion arose: that so-called free markets were best, and therefore the free-market concept should naturally include financial services—banks, S&Ls, mutual funds, brokerage houses, etc. This flew in the face of government-regulated safety, of course, but the overall assumption seemed to be that our financial institutions could cavort unfettered without endangering our collective life savings.

Well, it has not worked out that way. Under deregulation, financial service firms ran wild . . . crazy is a better word. Now we have options and futures, and options on futures, brackets, spreads and butterfly spreads. Interest rates, once stable, now gyrate like runaway rockets, and stock markets likewise have become totally bizarre.

The Elimination of Safeguards

Instead of adding safeguards to protect our life savings, the deregulation of the 1980s permitted just the opposite. Credit flew high, wide and handsome, with the devil left to take the hindmost.

Examples of this mindless mismanagement of the public's money were to be found in newly invented investment techniques and instruments which no longer prevented damage to one financial sector from spreading to another. The Chicago commodity markets, where for years agricultural products had been traded, added futures in financial instruments such as Treasury bills and bonds, and stock indexes, thus transforming itself into something of a gambling casino.

Modern technology made it possible for us to use home computers to deal in stocks and bonds and withdraw money without ever going near a bank. Trading on a twenty-four-hour-a-day basis around the world was initiated.

Previous banking barriers meant that farm banks loaned to farmers and oil banks to oilmen. With the breakdown of those barriers, banks all across America loaned to foreign countries, some of which the bankers had barely ever heard of and certainly had no real knowledge of.

Gyrating foreign exchange rates and unbalanced trade caused investors to seek more flexible means of savings—from interest-bearing checking accounts and variable rate mortgages to a whole panoply of options, futures, bond instruments and so forth.

There arose less and less distinction between types of borrowing and lending, between short-term and long-term, between national and international. With the barriers down, banks and investment houses were at each other's territorial throats to hawk their wares around the globe, twenty-four hours a day.

Financial Supermarkets

The battle cry became "Think Big!" And it was supposed that this was a brave new world in which proponents could trade just about anything, from houses and insurance policies to portfolios of stock . . . from an option on stock market futures to commercial paper borrowings convertible from debt to equity. And currencies could be swapped around the world at the touch of a button.

Bankers, brokers and financial whizzes thought this was a splendid idea. No longer did money have to be channeled through specific markets and separate institutions by particular financial houses. S&Ls, which had been kept strictly to the task of accepting our personal savings and making long-term mortgage loans were free to frolic in the money bazaar along with banks and brokerage firms. Stockbrokers, who hitherto had made careful distinctions between issues and firms, could sell junk bonds and invest huge sums in them to prop up the market. Banks, which had acted as depositories and lenders, got into speculating billions of dollars a day whether the yen or the S&P 500 would rise or fall.

In this new wonderland of financial markets, short-term borrowings were automatically rolled over to become medium-term financing. Bonds were readily converted into stocks. Interest and principal payments were separated and esoteric payback schemes originated.

In brief, it was a world in which no one could assess the risk in case something went wrong . . . as it always does, eventually.

Finance is not like any other industry. This is because it dramatically impacts everyone's well-being. Historically, it was therefore treated by governments as something special. Which is why we inherited the specialized financial institutions of the past. It's that specialization that was ended by deregulation.

By 1987 the world flow of funds and sale of U.S. government debts demanded that much of this debt fall into the hands of foreigners. As of late 1986, foreigners held close to $200 billion in U.S. Treasury debt. This was hailed as "free-market finance" by the yuppie generation.

In reality, what it has brought, silently and hardly noticed, is volatility and danger to every American pocketbook.

While all this deregulation was having its impact, the public, badly informed, was curiously detached. Loans to Latin American countries were thought of as dealings between banks and banana republics. What the public did not realize is that the banks were lending out their (read: yours and mine) money. And they were lending it to nations which had never repaid in the past and had no way of repaying in the future.

Thus the urgency now is to get your funds out of banks and S&Ls and into federal government-guaranteed instruments which you can personally manage without the intervention of stockbrokers, real estate operators, bankers or anyone else. The financial services industry is a disaster waiting to happen.

FINANCIAL CORPORATION OF AMERICA

This disaster has already cast its shadow. In 1984 the Financial Corporation of America (FCA) almost brought down the entire U.S. banking system. FCA was America's largest savings and loan with over $34 billion in assets, and had been badly managed—for the personal enrichment of its officers, led by Charles W. Knapp. Regulators ousted him in August 1984. The *Los Angeles Times*, quoting the new president in an article dated February 22, 1987, said, "If we had failed, there would be no FSLIC."

The new president and his henchmen then

went ahead and bet $34 billion that interest rates would continue to fall, or at least stay stable. They survived 1984 by borrowing heavily on Wall Street and from the Home Loan Board (a so-called regulatory agency). They fired 7,500 employees, sold their nine jet airplanes, dumped 732 cars they'd leased . . . and managed to lose another $700 million in bad loans in 1986.

In 1987 their total problem loans were close to $2 billion. Yet, believe it or not, S&L regulators gave permission for this corporation, with its growing mass of sick paper, to puff its assets from $27 billion at the end of 1985 to $34 billion by the end of 1986.

How was that achieved? By relabeling bundles of mortgages and having Wall Street dispose of these new securities to pension funds, insurance companies and other smart investors. The regulators said they had no choice: it was either let FCA continue to make bad loans or let it sink.

FCA is by no means a special case. To generate new funds, other lenders have taken to cutting their interest rates on fifteen-year fixed rate loans and selling them as "slam dunks" for new business. A lot of financial whizzes have put their clients into this piece of real estate action. And those "slam dunks" are going to be tombstones for billions of dollars when the coming hard times bring down real estate prices.

By the spring of 1985 the U.S. credit bubble had waxed bigger than the full moon. And just as surely as it waxed, it would wane—or, perhaps, combust and shrivel, leaving us to root through the ashes for our precious savings.

What to Do

So the question arises, "What can I do now to protect myself from the inevitable financial debacle?"

And with that, another question, "How can I take advantage of the bargain-basement opportunities the crash will bring?"

First of all, if you persist in believing that Uncle Sam is going to bail you out, or anyone else out, forget it. There is no insurance program in force that will ultimately return your money to your hands. Nor is there any prevention against the domestic social violence that will erupt when financial chaos descends. Nor any way to quickly fix the breakdown in communications and transportation.

During the early months of the Great Depression, just about everything that could go wrong did go wrong. And now, in the 1980s, there's a whole lot more that can go wrong. Practically everything is hooked up by electronics and computers, so what can go wrong this time will likely go wrong with the speed of light.

Second, remember that change is an ordeal. The coming change will be more of an ordeal than previous changes because of its sheer size. It will be far more than financial and economic. It will be political and social, too, for we have reached a watershed in American history. Tomorrow will present a totally new world, which we will have to learn to cope with and fashion a life from. This will be no mere replay of the past. It will be a greater transformation than anything in memorable history.

What you can do immediately—assuming you are reading this before the crash—is get your money out of banks and S&Ls. Don't wind up among the panicked crowd banging on the bank's closed door.

Also, get your money out of the stock market and out of mutual funds or money-management funds.

Do not keep more than a bare-bones balance in your bank or S&L, just enough to make a month's worth of bill payments.

Do not keep money in pension funds, retirement funds or life insurance policies, either. All these institutions invest your money in stocks and bonds and mortgages. Those financial instruments will be hit the hardest, so cash out before it's too late.

To secure your nest egg, buy U.S. three-month Treasury bills or U.S. savings bonds. The bills are in $10,000 denominations and the savings bonds may be bought for as little as $25. Buy them from your bank's Trust Department or from a stockbroker. The reason this is important is that while all else in the economy can be allowed to disintegrate, the U.S. Treasury will have to be held together at all costs. Without a federal foundation there is nothing at all left. And nothing to rebuild on.

Municipal Bonds

This is a favorite haven of everyone because of tax-free income. Present tax law changes alter this wonderful world, but aside from that, cash out of municipals because of a far greater danger: defaults! During the 1930s one of the worst places to have your money was in city and state bonds since so few could honor them. Today there is $1 trillion of this "paper" out there. Cash out now!

All About Yields

Everyone wants a high income and this means high interest rate returns that line your pockets. This is especially true of senior citizens living on fixed incomes. They have an imperative to maximize their cash flows with high yields. This is unfortunate.

A high yield carries with it a high risk. Recently I talked with someone who told me, with some pride, that he still had some big money in a S&L that had been paying him 16-1/2% for 6 years! I suggested that he forget it: S&L's are the worst places in the country to deposit and leave funds because many are insolvent and one day the whole business will go up in smoke. You must be cautious: if you lose your capital, you have no yield, and you are then truly up against it. So, forget yield. Look for capital safety above all!

U.S. Treasury Obligations

Right now the best place for large sums of money is 3- to 6-month U.S. Treasury bills. U.S. Treasury notes and bonds will fall dramatically in price. The bills will, too, but not as far. In addition, you can double your money in Treasury bonds at the right time, which is in motion and coming our way.

Corporate Bonds

Get out! Too risky.

Certificates of Deposit

Get out! A CD is no better than the bank or S&L that issued it and most of them are in trouble now!

FDIC & FSLIC Insurance

The FSLIC is insolvent. The FDIC has less than one cent for every $1 you have on deposit. Do not think for a second that the government will ride to the rescue of these deposit liabilities, as many believe. This is because the government must borrow the funds for such a rescue. This increases their debts, which are already sky high, and you would simply pay for this folly as a taxpayer. Not only that; if they even tried such a rescue they would wreck the bond market in the process since foreign holders of U.S. bonds would cash out and destroy bond prices. There is no fast and easy solution to this coming nightmare.

Gold

Start now buying gold coins, any kind, and hoarding them. Keep them at home, not in a safe deposit box at a bank (banks will be closed, and deposit box contents are not insured). Gold will rise to $2,000 an ounce and the bad news is that it will fall back to $35 an ounce. This is because the purchasing power of gold is always constant: one ounce buys a man's suit of clothes; in 1935 $35 gold bought a good suit; today $450 gold buys a good suit. You cannot have a fortune in gold and hope for super-low prices for the things you buy.

Silver

It will rise to over $100 an ounce, and then will fall, too.

What do you do if you have large profits in gold and silver? How do you preserve your gains? My suggestion is buy land in the country with your profits. Land, of course, will be very cheap as we get further into the depression, less than ten cents on the dollar for most everything.

Life Insurance Proceeds

Cash them out now while you can. Why? Insurance companies will take large losses in stocks and bonds and real estate, and pass them on to you. I know this since I worked for a major life insurance company as an economist years ago and saw the debris the Great Depression left. Also, AIDS will finish them off for good.

Pension Funds

Pray a lot if you are collecting one. These funds are managed by yuppie whizzes on Wall Street who are up to their eyeballs in stocks and bonds—paper that will vanish. If your pension fund survives, which is doubtful, it will then be cut.

The stock market crash of October 1987 directly affected many pension funds, especially those that invested in corporate stocks. Corporate pension funds generally invest 50% of their pension funds in stocks, 35% in corporate bonds, and the balance in real estate, certificates of deposit, etc.

It is only prudent to find out just where your pension fund has your money invested, and if it is not totally in Treasury bills, try to change this as soon as possible.

Military Retirement Pay and Social Security Income

Both of these will be reduced at least by half, maybe more. But the prices of the items you buy will also fall by that amount, so your purchasing power will be the same.

Above all, you must preserve your capital so you will have purchasing power and income as the economy is stood on its financial head. The good days are gone forever, perhaps, and we are all going to have to do a lot of surviving so you might get ready for this now.

The large fortunes in America, many of them, were made in hard times or depressions, when the wise and thrifty had funds and bought cheap. In the coming depression everything will be for sale, but few will have saved resources.

When Will the Panic Break Out?

No one knows when the final, major financial panic will happen. The time is not now that important, but being prepared is crucial. You must be ready. After the crash, it will be too late: you will be licked financially, filled with fear, and unable to cope. I caution you: be prepared. This advice is conservative, but it has stood the test of history for generations and it will tomorrow, too.

FUTURE BARGAINS IN REAL ESTATE

Always, in severe deflations, opportunities for real estate buys emerge at bargain basement prices. In Chicago in 1832 during a real estate crisis, a $15,000 house depreciated to $100 in one year.[1] In Florida in the late 1920s a real estate credit bubble grew and then burst, as all credit bubbles do, and beachfront property fell to one cent on the dollar. The more palatial the property is, the cheaper it will be since no one wants to get involved with property having high maintenance costs.

But to take advantage of these real estate buys, you must be *liquid.* If you are in dicey credit paper, like a certificate of deposit, you stand to lose much of its face value. This makes hoarding gold and silver coins rather attractive, doesn't it?

The October crash signaled a major reversal in the economy. Until then, the farm, oil, bank and thrift losses and commercial real estate losses had not totally impacted the mind of the public. For some unknown reason, the public maintained an uncanny optimism about the future.

The Stage Is Now Set

This is the time to batten down your financial hatches and get yourself personally prepared for financial survival. Be self-reliant because no one else will take care of you or protect you, and that includes Uncle Sam, who will have his hands filled, too, with tax revenue losses and larger-than-believable federal deficits and other unique problems.

For those with an eye to the future, the silver lining and the strategy is to secure your nest egg and patiently await the profit opportunities that always accompany hard times. As in the past most of the public will be caught by surprise, and left standing in a line at the bank. But someone has to be positioned to put Humpty Dumpty back together again. Begin now to become that somebody.

CONCLUSION

In this book I have to give you my vision of the dawn. And my views of our financial/economic realities are a far cry from conventional wisdom. How deeply these myths are entrenched came home to me in the fall of 1986 when I visited a friend in northern California and met a young woman attending one of California's many state universities. When she learned I was an economist, she promptly told me she was studying economics and that she knew the Federal Reserve controlled the money supply. I asked, "How so?" She explained, "Well, the Federal Reserve, through its open market operations, can increase or decrease bank reserves. And banks can borrow, when in need, from the Fed discount window, and the Fed can raise or lower the reserve requirements and thus control reserves. That's how they do it."

Her statement took me back twenty years to the time when I was teaching the same notions that are now found in modern economic and banking textbooks. Why do these myths persist? Obviously, many people have a vested interest in continuing down this blind alley. But historically, 1929 saw the same dichotomy with prevailing economic and banking notions popular in those times. History repeats but not exactly.

In the fall of 1986, too, history came back to confront us. A conservative president had gotten into trouble, but before the stock market crash. In 1929 Hoover was ruined after the crash. In 1986 Wall Street scandals surfaced before the crash; in 1929 they came to light after the crash. Banks all over America were falling like flies in 1985 and 1986, before the crash. In 1929, they fell afterward. So history walks on.

The Credit Structure

From the nature of credit, it is to be expected that a certain line will divide the views of creditors and debtors. The irrational fact is that since the early 1970s both debtors and lenders have pursued the same deceptions. As we will soon see (if we haven't already) the folly of the lender has exceeded the extravagance of the borrower. This became very evident in 1986 when General Motors, in its effort to sell more cars, lowered the interest rate on financing to 2.9% through its subsidiary, General Motors Acceptance Corporation (GMAC). It thus encouraged the least creditworthy to borrow, since it's safe to assume that consumers with shaky credit ratings were turning in their clunkers for new cars. The circle will be complete when GMAC is forced to repossess.

We have always believed in America that the panacea for debt is credit. Since 1975 most of what was called recovery was fueled by credit. We attracted debt problems by extending more credit. The result will be, if it's not already, the problem of how to pay back all this borrowed money.

Everyone in America seems to believe that just because he is an American, he is automatically entitled to the good life. As Garet Garrett wrote in 1932,

"If he cannot afford this out of his present income, credit must provide the good life. The assumption apparently is that if the standard of living is raised by credit, then people will be better creditors, better consumers, better to live with and better able to pay their debts willingly."

He continued,

"The result is that much of America is either bankrupt or in acute distress, having overborrowed according to this gospel. And we shall soon be witness to the failure of credit, and the falling living standards that go along with this 'discovery.'

"This will bring political and social upheaval. We will hear, in fact we're already hearing, that the government is in jeopardy. How will the government survive without credit? How will people live as they have learned to live, and as they are entitled to live, without benefit of credit? Will we tell them to go back?

"They will not go back. They will rise first. This is the emotional rhetoric. But what this does not say is that what people are threatening to rise against is the payment of debt for credit devoured.

"When we live on credit beyond our means, the debt sooner or later overtakes us. If we tax ourselves in America to pay past debts, this means we all go back a little. If we repudiate debt, that is the end of credit.

"In this dilemma the ideal solution recommended to us for over fifteen years, even to the creditor, is more credit, more debt. Our brand name economists refer to this mode of financial salvation as adding liquidity to the system. Liquidity is more debt, of course, but somehow its crucial debt-point is missed."

Garrett wrote,

"We all believe that the prosperity we have seen for years and years is not only the invisible hand of the free market at play, but it is also the American way. This belief led us to believe that this prosperity we enjoyed was a product of credit. From the beginning of economic thought, it has been supposed that the prosperity was from the increase and exchange of wealth, and credit was its product. But we had to all think in this upside-down, inside-out way. Our belief rationalized the belief as a whole.

"Perhaps the most astonishing imaginary process was in the field of international finance, where it became unorthodox to doubt that the use of credit in progressive magnitudes to inflate international trade and the problem of international debt would be solved. All debtor nations were going to meet their foreign obligations (for example, the Latin nations' $400 billion debt) from a favorable growing balance of trade.

"But we forgot: A nation's favorable balance in foreign trade is from selling more than it buys. Was it possible for nations to sell one another more than they bought from the others, so that every one should have a favorable trade balance? Certainly. But how? By selling on credit! By lending one another the credit to buy one another's goods. All nations would not be able to lend equally, of course. Each would lend according to its means, with the U.S. lending the most."[1]

As long as U.S. banks loaned ever increasing sums all over the world, it appeared that at long last prosperity was at hand. Then in 1974 world prices started falling, and by 1980–81 U.S. banks stopped lending mainly to Latin nations, then to other countries. It is an old rule in credit that unless a country is loaned enough to make its interest payments, it will, sooner rather than later, be in trouble. As in 1982 Mexico appeared with hat in hand to announce she was virtually bankrupt and would default.

A massive bank rescue was originated which, of course, left Mexico more in debt!

As the international situation intensified financially, the historical chestnut of trade barriers (protectionism) was again raised. This was more to lead us to believe that tariff barriers would ruin foreign trade, not bank-credit inflation, not the absurdity of attempting by credit to create a total of international exports greater than the sum of international imports so that every country could have a favorable balance out of which to pay its debts—with everyone wanting to sell without buying.

Trade Deficits

By late 1986 every American who knew anything at all about trade deficits "knew" that Uncle Sam's record deficits were caused by a weak dollar on the foreign exchange markets. That, according to popular wisdom, was why the Japanese and Germans were wrecking American manufacturing industries, and why the Rust Belt was in deep trouble with shutdowns and rising unemployment. Well, popular wisdom was wrong again.

The reason was because a huge spider web of debt had reappeared in foreign trade. Dr. Alfred J. Watkins wrote in *Till Debt Do Us Part,*

"There is an immediate and strong correlation between the Latin American $390 billion debt crisis and the rising U.S. trade deficits. Between 1977 and 1982 the U.S.

merchandise trade deficit moved in a narrow range. It dropped to a low of $36 billion in 1980, and rose to a high of just over $42 billion in both 1978 and 1982. In the three years since the onset of the debt crisis, the U.S. merchandise trade deficit rose dramatically. The U.S. posted a record $106 billion merchandise trade deficit in 1984. In 1985, the deficit was $117 billion."

In 1986, it was nearly $160 billion and was about $150 billion in 1987. Dr. Watkins continues,

"The link between the debt crisis and the U.S. trade deficit shows up most clearly in U.S. export statistics. Between 1980 and 1983, total U.S. exports declined by $20 billion, falling from $220.7 billion to $200.5 billion. During this period, U.S. exports to Mexico declined by $6 billion, exports to Brazil fell by $1.7 billion . . . Six major Latin American nations reduced their combined imports from $68.9 billion in 1980 to $42.4 billion in 1983. During this same period, U.S. exports to all of Latin America declined by $14 billion. In other words, 70% of the worldwide decline in U.S. overseas sales can be attributed to falling demand in Latin America, and 55% of Latin America's $26 billion in export reductions came at the expense of U.S. producers.

"Lower U.S. exports were rapidly converted into rising U.S. unemployment . . . most of these dwindling export opportunities are concentrated . . . in the smoke-stack industries.

"One of the reasons U.S. agricultural exports fell so sharply is that 15% of their export costs represented interest payments, and made them non-competitive. The cost of producing one ton of wheat in Argentina is less than $50 compared to $110 in America . . . Latin farmers have little debt, although their governments are heavily indebted to the U.S."

The Rising Dollar

Dr. Watkins notes:

"Although it may seem ironic, a rising dollar is the second way in which the U.S. provides global financial markets with enough dollars to pay interest on dollar denominated debt. In effect, a rising dollar ensures that U.S. products will be less competitive in world markets, and that foreign products will be more competitive in U.S. markets. The result of this changing international price structure is a rapidly increasing U.S. trade deficit. A U.S. trade deficit with Latin America is a necessary by-product of the debt crisis, as well as a precondition for providing debtor nations with dollars to pay interest. The emerging argument as to whether American taxpayer dollars should contribute to the resolution of the international debt crisis overlooks the less direct, but no way less real, ways in which Americans are already bearing the burden of the crisis. Life has been made much more difficult for workers and businesses who depend on exports or who are sensitive to rising levels of imports."[2]

So the debt chickens come home to roost in various disguises. Surrounding all this is a question: Why have mainstream economists and politicians not revealed this other side of the debt? Why do they minimize debts in general and only stress federal deficits? Why do they ignore the much larger private-debt pyramid?

Their reasoning seems to go back before John Law and his Mississippi Scheme. Garet Garrett concluded,

"The belief that debt need never be paid, that it may be infinitely postponed, that a creditor nation may pay itself by progressively increasing the debts to its debtors. This is the logic of the credit delusion. The principle is quite simple. You have only to find a way to multiply your creditors by the cube and pay them by the square, out of their own money. Then, for a while, you are in command—1 fish cut up for bait brings 3. Two cut up for bait bring 8, the cube of 2. Four bring 64 and 16 bring 4,096, while 256, the square of 16, brings 16,771,216. "When the delusion breaks, people, all with one impulse, hoard their money. Banks, all with one impulse, hoard credit, and debt becomes debt again. Credit is ruined. Suddenly there is not enough for daily needs. Yet only a short time before we had been saying and thinking there was a great surplus of American credit and the only thing we could do was export the OPEC surplus balance of the 1970s. How absurd it sounds in echo. How absurd it was in the first place."[3]

The central problem for the economy and for all Americans in the days ahead will be to find enough credit to perform the works that are in sight: unemployment benefits, welfare, etc. We can already see that much of America needs new capital to take the place of wornout old capital. The $1 trillion deficit in infrastructure (roads, sewers, water systems we have ignored for twenty years) is a prime example. This is the tip of a very large iceberg. Finally, our standard of living will fall and, uniquely in our history, our major money center banks and their owners will be facing trouble.

In all previous American crises the big banks and their owners managed to come through unscathed. But this time it is different. The big banks have loaned out their wealth and the assets of millions of small depositors as well. So everyone will be, or is, caught up in this financial failure.

The stage will be set for something new. Our tomorrow will be very different from the tomorrow faced by policymakers in 1933. But Americans will hunker down, do without, do the job required to retrieve that of our past which is retrievable. And that is a very bullish thought for us all.

Credit Securitization: Creating Funny Money

I have stressed in this book that credit—the lifeblood of our capitalistic system—has always been a problem in our society because of both its use and abuse. I have given chapter and verse about how most of it is created outside the control of the Federal Reserve, the U.S. Treasury or any other government entity.

Even today this idea is poorly understood. But Marriner Eccles, Chairman of the Federal Reserve all during the Great Depression, understood this and wrote about it. He said, "The commercial banks are creators and destroyers of money (credit) without being recognized by the people or the government as creators and destroyers of money."

I have also noted that the increased creation of credit is not always inflationary. Most times it is deflationary because liabilities are created simultaneously. What must be emphasized is this: the creation of credit always carries with it interest which is compounded, making the debt, most times, unrepayable.

I've also pointed out that, in general, economic activity peaked in the world (and in the U.S.) in 1973, marking the onset of a one hundred and twenty-five-year cycle (from trough to trough and from peak to peak), according to Fernand Braudel. All during the ongoing slow-down, which began in 1973, new and frightening forms of credit continue to be created by the private sector.

This became a bona-fide financial revolution, with free-wheeling credit creation by the private sector, violating every historical rule of sagacity and thrift.

SECURITIZATION!

In the early 1980s the word "securitization" became Wall Street's euphemism for the funny money game being played. What does the word mean?

Henry Kaufman, Chief Economist for Salomon Brothers, the New York investment firm, described the process of securitization as "one which transfers obligations (debt) from non-marketable to marketable." How was this done?

Well, the Bank of America, for one, sold off $400 million worth of their credit-card credit to a financial services firm, and created a new debt which they then marketed to pension funds, insurance companies . . . maybe widows and orphans.

The historical truism involved here is this: consumer credit is the most unstable form of credit to get involved with, simply because consumers generally do not control their own financial destinies. Most consumers, if they lose their jobs and cannot get new jobs quickly, find that their credit-worthiness plummets.

So what Bank of America did was take those

debts off its books by spreading them to bigger risk takers.

It was estimated that in 1986 alone, new and varied forms of securitization totaled almost $700 billion.[4] The most noteworthy and stable form of this was the bundling of home mortgages into packages. This was done by federal government agencies, who then had new securities to sell, with mortgages as collateral.

Buyers of these new securities were assured of a steady cash flow as homeowners made their payments. In 1986 that cash flow was $600 billion, "larger than the total volume of loans outstanding made by all the commercial banks to all the nation's businesses."[5]

As early as 1985, the financial experts were busy packaging car loans, lease receivables and so on. The ingenuity of financial men is something to reckon with! For example, General Motors Acceptance Corporation (GMAC) alone had originated more than $7 billion of securitized car loan issues in 1985-86. It was estimated that by the end of 1986, securitized car loans outstanding would total more than $10 billion.

Why was this done?

In order to keep the funny money game going.

The vast $11 trillion credit cloud that hangs over all our heads was springing leaks. Losses by oilmen, farmers and commercial real estate holders were mounting. The credit bubble had begun to shrink. So it became imperative to create still more credit. The fact that this new credit would be conjured up with less equity was of no concern. "Keep the game going" was the credo.

Mind you, this shakier form of credit has purchasing power just like any other form of credit has. Again, there were no government controls or entries into this process, although the President of the Federal Reserve Bank of New York, in the Annual Report for 1986, cautioned:

> "The rapid growth of securitization is having a profound impact on the credit organization process in the U.S. and elsewhere . . . As it grows, the size and implications of contingent claims on financial institutions and the capacity of the system to 'work out' problems will come under question."[6]

What he meant was, there is a lot more at risk now.

The Madness of the Crowd

I began this book with reference to the growing irrationality, irresponsibility and madness of the U.S. financial system, and its parallel with the South Sea Bubble and other past manias. We, like they, wish to believe we have come up with something truly new and creative, and that our system has safeguards. But we, like they, were wrong. History marches on.

By early 1987 the entire U.S. financial system was being driven by sentiment, emotion, and not by prospective profits or good economic news. It was the very same sentiment which drove prices up during the era of the South Sea

Company and John Law's Mississippi scheme in 1720—the sentiment which had people believing that gold mines in Mississippi and Louisiana would provide rich profits for shareholders.

Historically, we are just closing the circle. We have gone, since 1945, from an era of real economic growth, inflation, easy credit and a rising mania, into closing the circle with economic contraction, tight credit and a savage deflationary period which will erupt, as it always has in the past, with a massive financial panic. Only the sets, costumes and names of the key actors change—the same old drama repeats.

The expansion of the meaning of securitization beyond its traditional meaning (home mortgages guaranteed by government agencies) brought two major changes: (1) it increased the tendencies of the big borrowers to sell their securities to investors (sometimes even with a back-up line of credit from a bank, carrying idiocy to its extreme) instead of going to a bank to get a loan; and (2) it added to the banks' own propensity to convert the loans they had made (credit cards, cars, etc.) into marketable securities.

These led, in turn, to the growth of financial topsy-turviness. Backup bank lines of credit, including note-insurance facilities, rose to $33 billion by 1986. The commercial paper market in the U.S. by late 1986 had doubled to almost $350 billion in five short years. The New York investment bank, Salomon Brothers, estimated that new issues of asset-based securities (those backed by mortgages, car loans, credit card loans) amounted to almost $270 billion in 1986, up from about $125 billion in 1980.[7]

The second trend blurring into the first was the proliferation of new financial instruments. This became a large pile of paper ranging from junk bonds to floating-rate notes to swaps (agreements to exchange interest rate or currency obligations, etc.). These were new ways of distributing risk. The numbers were also big: $135 billion in junk bonds, $300 billion in interest rate swaps, $40 billion in currency swaps, and $680 billion in open positions in financial futures and options.

What was the true degree of risk in all this? We will soon see. You can spread risk, but you cannot get rid of it. Like the old Joe Louis saying, "He can run, but he can't hide." And so it will be when the bell tolls on this big pyramid of paper.

It seems to me that the banks were playing a fool's game with our money. They had no familiarity with trying to assess market risk. Their forte, supposedly, was assessing credit risk, the risk of default. Market risk was something else entirely.

Securitization also put the investment banks into the business of extending credit directly by pledging their own capital in leveraged corporate buyouts. I feel strongly that this idea of spreading more specific risks among more participants will prove fatal. We shall see.

Too much risk has been shouldered by financial institutions. For example, the U.S. savings and loan industry accumulated 15% of the total junk bonds sold. If the issuers of those junk bonds get into trouble, the S&L industry—already a basket case—will fail utterly.

The problem has been, and continues to be, that risk takers themselves don't know the risks. And their array of new financial inventions simply had too many bells and whistles for anyone to really understand what was going on. And we will find, if we haven't already, that the thing they all lacked in the moment of truth can be summed up in one word. *Liquidity.*

EPILOGUE

A World Bewitched

It is one thing to have the credit system destroyed, but following hard upon this will be the deeper-lying destruction of social morale, and this takes a little longer. Up until this crisis our system was maintained by the general good behavior of common men, by the honesty and punctuality of clerks, workers of all sorts: traders, lawyers, the butcher, the baker, etc. The one thing we revere most, but rarely acknowledge, is *security*, and this depends on the habitual decent behavior of all of us in the street and in the country. The average man behaved well because he had faith that his pay was safe, if sometimes scanty, and he felt some assurance of a certain comfort and dignity in his life. He imagined an implicit bargain between himself and society that he should be given employment and security in exchange for his law-abiding subordination, and that society would keep faith with his savings. He was not a good boy for nothing. Nobody is. But now the average man will have to face financial distress, his savings gone, and he will naturally ask himself whether it paid to be industrious and law-abiding. The cement of confidence in our social fabric since 1945 has been on the decline and turning to dust. This is evident in the steadily rising crime figures and prison population.

So now we come to a halt. As surely as night follows day, this will bring social chaos and human travail. We must prepare ourselves for that dilemma. The immense inertia of the old order, the old way of things, will be gone. At first we will see dismayed apprehension, like a chilly stillness that comes at times before the breaking of a storm. The millions of future unemployed will become more plainly a challenge *and then a menace.*

FOOTNOTES

Preface
1. Juglar, Clement. *Des Crises Commerciales.* Paris: 1889, p. 121.

Introduction
1. Walsh, David. *The Idea of Economic Complexity.* New York: Viking, 1984, p. 137.
2. Silk, Leonard. "Business Perspective," *New York Times,* January 2, 1985.
3. Council of Economic Advisors. *Economic Report of the President 1987.* Washington, D.C.
4. *New York Times,* March 6, 1984, p. 18.
5. Maken, John. *The Global Debt Crisis.* New York: Basic Books, 1984, p. 95.
6. "Economic Forecasting," *Time,* August 27, 1984, p. 18.
7. "Commodity Prices," *Wall Street Journal,* July 27, 1984.
8. Capy, Peter. Inyo, California *Register,* July 22, 1987.

Chapter 1

1. MacKay, Charles. *Extraordinary Popular Delusions and the Madness of Crowds.* New York: Harmony Books, 1979.

Chapter 2

1. Durant, Will & Ariel. *The Lessons of History.* New York: Simon & Schuster, 1968.
2. Braudel, Fernand. *Perspective of the World.* New York: Harper & Row, 1982, p. 87.
3. Eccles, Marriner, S. *Beckoning Frontiers.* New York: Alfred A. Knopf, 1951, p. 108.

Chapter 3

1. *Wall Street Journal,* November 15, 1977.
2. Organization European Community Development. *Staff Study.* 1972, p. 4.
3. *Wall Street Journal,* June 12, 1978.
4. Pigou, A. C. *The Economics of Welfare.* London: Cambridge University Press, 1920, pp. 833–844.
5. Private letter to author, April 15, 1977.
6. *Wall Street Journal,* December 21, 1977.
7. Gimpel, Jean. *The Medieval Machine.* New York: Holt, Reinhart & Winston, 1976, pp. 46–48.
8. Spengler, Oswald. *The Decline of the West,* Vol. 1. New York: Alfred A. Knopf, 1926, pp. 21–26.
9. King, John L. *Human Behavior and Wall Street.* Chicago, IL. Swallow Press, 1973, p. 30.
10. Gimpel, op.cit.. p. 62.

Chapter 4

1. Noyes, Guy E. *Morgan Guaranty Bank Survey,* October 1981, p. 7.
2. "Behind Reagan's Economic Shuffle," *New York Times,* January 13, 1985.
3. Robinson, Joan. *Classical and Neoclassical Theories of Equilibrium.* New York: Oxford University Press, 1979.

Chapter 5

1. American Institute of Banking. *Principles of Bank Operations.* New York: American Bankers Association, 1966, p. 316.
2. *Citibank Economic Week,* August 27, 1984.
3. Kindelberger, Charles. *Manias, Panics and Crashes.* New York: Basic Books, 1978, p. 55.

Chapter 6

1. Dorfman, Joseph. *The Economic Mind in American Civilization.* New York: Kelly, 1969, Vol. 4, p. 361.

Chapter 7

1. *Business Week,* February 15, 1988.
2. *Wall Street Journal,* February 8, 1988.
3. *Federal Reserve Bulletin.* Washington, D.C.: November 1936.
4. Caughey, Andrew. *Monthly Review,* February 1985, pp. 61–63.

Chapter 9

1. "Contracting the Economy," *Business Week,* September 30, 1970, p. 86.
2. *Business Week,* September 3, 1979, p. 102.

3. *Business Week*, October 11, 1982, pp. 126–130.
4. Veblen, Thorstein. *Theory of the Leisure Class*. New York: New American Library, 1954, p. 66.
5. Federal Reserve Board, *Federal Reserve Bulletin*, December 1986, pp. 23, 24, 27, 39; Mortgage Debt: *Economic Report of the President 1987*, 3rd Quarter, 1986, p. 328.
6. Haas, Gilbert, *General Review*, Summer 1987.

Chapter 12
1. Noyes, op. cit., p. 7.
2. *Business Week*, September 12, 1978, p. 28.
3. "The Death of Equities," *Business Week*, August 13, 1979, p. 76.

Chapter 13
1. Buch, Norman S. *Survey of Contemporary Economics*.

Chapter 14
1. Silk, Leonard. "Optimistic Fiscal Forecasts," *Daily Commerce*, November 23, 1987.

Chapter 15
1. Braudel, op. cit., pp. 78–88.

Chapter 16
1. Lessinger, Jack. *Regions of Opportunity*. New York: Times Books, p. 212.

Conclusion
1. Garrett, Garet. *A Bubble That Broke the World*. Boston: Little Brown & Co., 1932, pp. 4, 5, 6, 29.

2. Watkins, Albert J. *Till Debt Do Us Part.* Washington, D.C.: Roosevelt Center for Policy Studies, 1986, pp. 10–11.
3. Garrett, op.cit., p. 37.
4. Federal Reserve Bank of Kansas City. *Economic Review*, December 1986.
5. Bryan, Lowell L. "The Credit Bomb in Our Financial System," *Harvard Business Review*, January/February 1987.
6. *Annual Report 1986*, Federal Reserve Bank of New York.
7. *The Economist*, March 21, 1987, p. 64.

BIBLIOGRAPHY

Adams, Brooks. *The Law of Civilization and Decay.* New York: Alfred A. Knopf, 1912.

American Institute of Banking. *Principles of Banking.* New York: American Banking Association, 1936.

Angell, Norman. *The Story of Money.* New York: Frederick A. Stokes, 1929.

Bressand, Albert. *The State of the World Economy.* New York: Harper & Row, 1982.

Cassell, Francis. *Gold or Credit?.* New York: Frederick A. Praeger, 1967.

Denison, Edward. *Accounting for Economic Growth 1929–1969.* Washington, D.C.: Brookings Institution, 1974.

Dorfman, Joseph. *The Economic Mind in American Civilization, Vol. 4.* New York: Kelly, 1969.

Douglas, Paul. *Controlling Depressions.* New York: W. W. Norton, 1935.

Durant, Will and Ariel. *The Lessons of History.* New York: Simon & Schuster, 1968.

Eccles, Marriner, S. *Beckoning Frontiers.* New York: Alfred A. Knopf, 1951.

Fisher, Irving. *The Theory of Interest.* New York: Macmillian, 1964.

Friedman, M. & Shwartz, Anna. *The Monetary History of the U.S.* Princeton, N.J.: Princeton University Press, 1977.

Galbraith, John K. *The Great Crash.* Boston: Houghton, Mifflin, 1961.

Goldenweiser, E. A. *Monetary Management.* New York: McGraw-Hill, 1949.

Groseclose, Elgin. *Money and Man.* Norman, Okla.: University of Oklahoma Press, 1934.

Hansen, Alvin H. *Business Cycles and National Income.* New York: W.W. Norton, 1951.

Homer, Sidney: *A History of Interest Rates.* New Brunswick, N.J.: Rutgers University Press, 1963.

Jacoby, N. H. *U.S. Monetary Policy.* New York: Praeger, 1934.

Jastrow, Roy W. *The Golden Constant.* New York: Wiley, 1977.

Kindelberger, Charles. *Manias, Panics & Crashes.* New York: Basic Books, 1978.

Kindelberger, Charles. *The World in Depression 1929–1939.* Berkeley, CA.: University of California Press, 1973.

LeBon, Gustave. *The Crowd.* London: Ernest Benn, 1895.

Lekachman, Robert. *The Age of Keynes.* New York: Vintage, 1968.

Mackay, Charles. *Extraordinary Popular Delusions and The Madness of Crowds.* New York: Harmony Books, 1980.

Makin, John. *Global Debt Crisis.* New York: Basic Books, 1984.

Mitchell, W.C. *Business Cycles.* New York: National Bureau Economy Research, 1954.

Mitchell, W. C. *History of the Greenbacks.* Chicago, IL.: University of Chicago Press, 1903.

Myers, M. C. *Financial History of U.S.* New York: Columbia University Press, 1970.

National Industrial Conference Board. *The Banking Situation in the U.S.* New York: NICB, 1932.

Pechman, Joseph. *Federal Tax Policy.* Washington, D.C.: Brookings Institution, 1968.

Rostow, W.W. *The Stages of Economic Growth.* London, England: Cambridge University Press, 1960.

Salter, Sir Arthur. *Recovery—The Second Effort.* New York: Century, 1932.

Samuelson, Paul A. *Economics,* 11th ed. New York: McGraw-Hill, 1980.

Sweezy, Paul & Baran, Paul. *Monopoly Capital.* New York: Modern Reader, 1966.

Tobin, James. *The New Economics, One Decade Older.* Princeton, N.J.: Princeton University Press, 1974.

Toffler, Alvin. *The Third Wave.* New York: William Morrow, 1980.

Tuchman, Barbara. *The March of Folly.* New York: Alfred A. Knopf, 1984.

Twentieth Century Fund. *Debts & Recovery.* New York: Twentieth Century Fund, 1938.

Von Mises, Ludwig. *Human Action.* Chicago, IL.: Regnery, 1949.

Warren, G. T. & Pearson, F. A. *Gold and Prices.* New York: Wiley, 1935.

Wells, H. G. *The Outline of Man's Work and Wealth.* New York: Doubleday, 1931.

Wright, Conrad D. *Industrial Depressions 1886.* Washington, D.C.: U.S. Government Printing Office, 1968.

INDEX

JOHN L. KING, Ph.D., has helped small investors safeguard and build their nest eggs through his monthly newsletter, "Future Economic Trends," for over 17 years. Among his numerous outstanding predictions were the oil-price decline of the 1980s, the farm crisis, and the stock market crash of 1987.

When you finish reading this book, you'll be terrified, and electrified, and you'll feel as though you've come face-to-face with a prophet. . . .

Thousands of readers write Dr. King after reading his book, asking for even more ways to protect themselves and profit from the coming calamity. So Dr. King has fashioned a highly acclaimed newsletter called Future Economic Trends. Each month he fills FET with his most daring insights. He chronicles the collapse's advance, and shows readers how to take command of every area of their lives—from real estate to gold bullion and cash. He does so in a style that is as provocative and digestible as is this book.

If you're like most readers, you'll complete this book in a few fright-filled sittings. You'll sprint to the finish, hoping for some white knight to charge across the page and take control of our economic destiny.

But this is the real world, where government snafus worsen the crises, where politics reign king, and where only one man, Dr. John L. King, is capable of providing you the ongoing tools to be your own white knight, to seize control of your own little destiny, and to turn this crash into a profit opportunity the likes of which you've never seen before.

When you're through with this book, remember to turn back to this card. Like thousands of others, you'll want to become—You'll see that you really must become—one of Dr. King's faithful and lifelong disciples.

To order you subscription to Future Economic Trends, complete the short order form below and send it off today.

Here is my order:

☐ Check enclosed in the amount of $39.00

☐ Three month trial only $19.95

☐ Bill my credit card: ☐ VISA ☐ MasterCard ☐ American Express
        ☐ Diners ☐ Carte Blanche

Credit card number: _____ Exp. Date: _____

Signature _____

Name: _____

Address: _____

City/State/Zip: _____

Phone: (_____) _____

For immediate ordering call (800) 633-8112, #400

Then, send this registration form and your check or credit card authorization to: Future Economic Trends, P.O. Box 1550, Goleta, Ca. 93116